PROLOGUE

Life was good. Born into a tight-knit family with two loving parents and three wonderfully close siblings, I grew up in tony Westport, Conn., knowing little of trial or tribulation. Except for the anguish of being "dumped" by a serious wife prospect in my early twenties, I never had a life crisis – nothing even remotely resembling one. No deaths or traumas to deal with, no emotional or physical maladies to overcome, no parental or sibling conflicts to mess with or get messed up by. The worst abuse I ever suffered during those formative years involved beets and lima beans and a distasteful parental requirement that I actually eat them.

Life was easy, too. I was an honor student who earned my grades with little or no effort; a hard core jock who captained several teams; an unpromising thespian who nonetheless landed leading roles in school productions. An athlete, an actor, and straight? Many girls went for it! So did college admissions people. In 1974, I went off to Princeton. Upon graduation I joined IBM in its elite Data Processing Division; graduated No. 1 from its prestigious sales training program; bought a house with my best pal, my brother, on the Connecticut side of the Long Island Sound, which we shared with three renters for five years in fraternity-like, testosterone-driven social mayhem; married a woman I felt passionate about; had three incredible kids; jumped the IBM ship after 12 years and four moves to spend the next 18 with a start-up software company that went public in 1999 and made me millions…Well, at least on paper.

In short, life was perfect—except for one thing: I spent all these years wrapped tight in an emotionally protective cocoon. The "real" me was unavailable to the world at-large. More disastrously, the "real" me was unavailable to my wife. Worst of all, the "real" me was unavailable even to myself. It took a crisis of catastrophic proportion to shake me from my reverie—or perhaps I should say my fog.

I read somewhere that transformation is not a spectator sport; that at every crossroad in life we make the choice for greater or lesser awareness. Shortly after my 46th birthday and only days after my 19th wedding anniversary, I learned just what that meant. In the space of a week, my life got unceremoniously dumped in a blender set on high. It was like God, or whatever that bigger energy up there is, shouted in my ear, "You're not listening, Lewis, so here's a wake-up call you *can't* ignore."

The message came in the form of a shock bulletin from my wife. She was "disconnecting," she said. She was not in love with me anymore, indeed may *never* have been in love with me. She was tired and unhappy. If it weren't for our three kids, she told me, she'd move out right now. For me, her blunt message came out of left field. I thought we had an idyllic marriage. The prospect of an unforeseen divorce may not be earthshaking to many, but to me it was unthinkable.

I thought I had an idyllic job, too. But just days later, my job got redefined downwardly—a nice way of saying that I was demoted from a key executive position and principal in the company to field salesman. Having come in second in a battle with my boss, I now faced no prospect of making any money in the short term. This, no less, at a time when I was gonad-deep in a ridiculously expensive house renovation.

I THOUGHT WE WERE HAPPY

LESSONS MY WIFE TAUGHT ME
ON THE ROAD TO DIVORCE

BY: JONATHAN L LEWIS

ISBN: 1463750048
ISBN-13: 9781463750046

IN MEMORY OF MY SISTER, ANN (Pooz!) who did more living in her 51 years than any 51 one of us combined. You will *ALWAYS* be my inspiration.

TABLE OF CONTENTS

So much for good, easy, perfect. Now, my life was awful. Hard. A fucking mess.

I did what any reasonable man would do under the circumstances: I crumbled. I mean, I came *totally* apart. This was no small crisis – it was a nuclear explosion.

My ensuing transformation has been difficult, slow and excruciatingly painful. It's been a journey without boundaries, rules and, as of this writing, a final destination. Lonely and scary, this path of change has been marked by introspection, anxiety and depression. It's also been marked by growth and unexpected moments of clarity, carnality and catharsis.

This journey continues to be a work in progress—one that I now understand will persist, though I hope less brutally, to the end of my days. I have learned to welcome the attendant uncertainty, the examination, even the vulnerability that comes from "not knowing." Having found the courage to break out of my comfortable cocoon to explore who I am, I feel stronger, more receptive, more alive. But that courage hasn't—and often still doesn't—come easily. It's taken a lot of flailing and screaming and soaking in blatant self-pity to open myself up to the possibilities. For the longest time, the hurt cut so deep that I didn't think that I would ever move forward, heal or trust again.

Frankly, I didn't know guys go through shit like this. I guess that's why I'm sharing this story with you. To say to the men who might be going through similar stuff: It happens. Hang in there, it gets better. You're not alone. And to say to the women who are convinced that their mates inhabit a different planet: Yeah, we probably do at times, but rest assured the pain is no less intense, no less real.

At some point in our lives, we have to choose just how conscious we want to be. I lived the first 46 years of my life in a stupor. Now in my 50s, I am more aware of what it takes to achieve the intimacy and love that is as fundamental to my existence as food and air. Along the way, I have been fortunate to receive the guidance, support and instruction of family, friends, casual acquaintances, even total strangers. But ultimately, I've learned, the place that holds the answers—and the questions—is that loneliest and scariest place of all: within myself.

1. ONCE UPON A TIME

We were a perfect couple.

At least that's what I—and pretty much everyone who knew us—thought. When married friends would catch the two of us in the kitchen in our trademark pose, my arms encircling Kelly's back, Kelly's head pressed close against my chest, her hand gently patting my rib cage, they'd smile knowingly and say with a hint of a sigh, "Look at the two of you. You're so in love. How do you keep it so romantic after so many years?"

No doubt about it, we made an appealing pair: beautiful Kelly, diminutive and shapely, with bright blue-gray eyes and a knowing smile; me, gangly and well-toned, with trusting blue eyes and a goofy grin that floated a full foot above her head. Ours was a yin and yang that had a nice synergy. Where Kelly was thoughtful and introspective, I was a solution-oriented, get-the-job-done extrovert. She was a bit shy; I was garrulous. She offered a sympathetic ear; I provided the shot of adrenalin and humor. Kelly had a New Agey disposition that rubbed up nicely against my romantic streak. Her penchant for illuminating rooms with candles and playing soft music set the mood for my favorite activity: cuddling. Which we did. A lot. So often, in fact, that our three kids' most common refrain was, "Get a room!"

About those three kids: Kelly and I were on the same page. Always. Our two sons and daughter came first. Period. That was our central shared value, and from that, decisions about the shape our lives took together flowed effortlessly. Though we'd met as colleagues at IBM in the early '80s, she, at 27, a systems engineer, I, at 24, a salesman, we opted early-on in our marriage for a traditional lifestyle: she would keep the household running; I would keep the paychecks flowing. We both liked this arrangement. It gave me peace of mind that the kids could count on her being around; it gave Kelly more time to pursue her many creative interests. Despite her stay-at-home part of the bargain, ours was a modern marriage. I gladly did at least 50% of all chores. If she cooked, I cleaned. If I did the food shopping, which I did most of the time since she hated it, she did the sewing repairs which I could never get right. We kept no charts, needed no discussion about balancing household duties. I willingly participated in all of it: the laundry, carpooling, vacuuming, even ironing, though I'm not very good at that either. Until the kids began to hit puberty, neither of us thought of changing this status quo. It worked for us.

We must have exuded something special, because ours was a home that attracted a steady flow of visitors. Our adult friends felt comfortable dropping by without forewarning. The kids' friends treated our place like Grand Central Station, coming and going at all hours of the day and night. Where many of the other parents in Doylestown, PA, often didn't know where their kids were, we always knew where ours were: somewhere in the house—often hosting one of those kids who had gone AWOL. The traffic in and out of our home was so heavy that our driveway was a constant jam of cars, bikes and skateboards. No matter what the age of the driver, everyone knew they were welcome. The contents of our refrigerator were theirs for the taking; the open, easy flow of the house was theirs for the playing and our couches and beds were theirs for the crashing.

Ours was also the home relatives descended on. My three siblings' four kids and Kelly's older sister's two kids loved to come visit Uncle Jonathan and Aunt Kelly (or Aunt Penis, as my niece Emily called her back when she was a tot). Holidays at our house were easy. Lots of dogs and cats to frolic with. A pool to swim in. Plenty of hikes and fun activities. Tons of great food. Flexible bedtimes; few baths. Everyone knew Kelly made the best apple pie in the world; everyone knew I gave the best foot rubs.

Come the Jewish holidays, ours was a home fellow members of our local temple flocked to. We offered a mix of traditional and modern that made some of the more tedious aspects of Jewish observance go down easy. During the years I was the president of our synagogue, board meetings were pleasant, services were mercifully concise, intra-congregational squabbles were kept to a dull roar. When members butted heads, they knew they could work things out "in committee" at our house, where Kelly's hospitality was warm and sympathetic, and I, a bit impatient, a lot practical, helped to smooth things over.

Kelly and my well-trafficked, two-story brick home was an apt reflection of our marriage: loving, embracing, welcoming. Steady and reliable. Plainly, I wasn't alone in this perception. When Kelly's younger sister got gravely ill, ours was the place she often migrated to during her recuperation. When my older sister was bottoming out over infertility, ours was the home she felt comfortable retreating to in order to hide from the world a day here, a day there. Most telling, two of my siblings designated Kelly and me as the guardians of their kids; so did Kelly's older sister. If that's not a tribute to the life Kelly and I built together, I don't know what is.

Of course, not every minute of our marriage was perfect. We had our differences, sure. I, for instance, was raised to show up five minutes early to everything; Kelly has rarely been on time for anything in her life. I was raised to put things away; Kelly favors a more relaxed, cluttered approach. My idea of unwinding is to let my mind go blank at the end of an arduous day; Kelly prefers probing conversations that last until dawn. Sometimes when our different styles rubbed against each other, we would collide. But our fights were brief and contained. Worst case, they lasted a few hours, maybe followed by a day or three of uncomfortable silence. During those times, I was incapable of offering a loving response or trying to understand where Kelly was coming from. For me, it was easier to withdraw, let the tension settle in my gut, make like our fight wasn't happening. If Kelly tried to initiate dialogue before my internal storm abated, I would straight-arm her emotionally. I would often give her the silent treatment or fling a few terse words, making it clear that I wasn't in any mood for conversation to cover for my own insecurities and inability to handle the tension. I know now that I brandished silence largely to cover it. It wasn't the most mature approach. But it was all I knew how to do. Besides, I also knew the stress would pass. And by the time it did, I usually found it painless to put my arms around her and apologize.

So, I thought, did she. Certainly, she made it seem that way as we hugged and kissed and cleared the air. Each time I walked away from one of these low-level battles, I had the sense that she'd hated being estranged from me as much as I'd hated being at odds with her.

As the years of our marriage ticked by, my love for my bride grew only stronger, deeper, more certain. I'm a hugger from the word go, and the longer I was married to Kelly, the more I couldn't keep my hands off of her. For me, there weren't enough opportunities in the day to say, "I love you." When I was at work, I couldn't call home enough times each day, every day, to hear the sound of her voice.

Plain and simple, I adored my wife. Her steady reciprocation of my affection made me feel content, comfortable, complacent, confident. I regarded her as my intimate, my best friend, the rainmaker who showered happiness on my life every day. During the first 19 years of our marriage, it never occurred to me—not once—that she might feel otherwise.

Boy, was I a dumb schmuck.

The first warning shot was fired in August. Or at least the first one I heard.

It came on a Saturday morning, one week after our 19th wedding anniversary. At that moment in time, our usually tranquil home life was being rocked by a double whammy: a top-to-bottom renovation of our house, and a job assignment that was keeping me up in Portsmouth, N.H., most days of the work week. So, when Kelly and I awoke before the kids, and she suggested we go out for coffee, I assumed this was an invitation to steal some time alone together. We liked to do that, make time for just us.

I don't remember what we were talking about as we bought some bagels and coffee in town, then settled at an outdoor table. I'd awakened unrested from my heavy work week and travel schedule; my lower back was giving me fits again. What I do recall is glancing at my watch through bleary eyes and realizing that our daughter had to be somewhere at 10:00. Abruptly, I stood up and said, "Let's go, or we'll be late for Sarah."

"I'm not ready to go yet," Kelly responded tensely. "I haven't finished my bagel."

"We're gonna be late," I snapped.

Too tired and achy to back down, I said she was trying to prove something by not leaving, and I didn't like it. She, in turn, made it clear that she didn't like being told what to do. "I'm not telling you what to do, damn it," I said. "It's just not fair to Sarah to be late. Let's *go.*"

I was so shut off from reality, so clueless about the turmoil between us, that it seemed a small event, an inconsequential exchange. It proved to be the proverbial straw that broke Kelly's back. "I'm sick of your irritability," she growled. "I'm tired of you barking out orders."

"I just don't want to be late for Sarah," I persisted. "What's the big freakin' deal?"

"Do you know what you're doing? Do you know where you're pushing me? You know that poster in the chiropractor's office— the picture of the frayed rope with only one fiber left holding it together? That's where I am right now. I'm that close to completely losing it with you. I'm hanging on by one fragile thread. I can't take it any more."

Huh? I stared at my wife blankly. Jesus, couldn't she see I was just tired and cranky? Didn't she have any sympathy for my corkscrewed back? Why was she making such a fuss? I felt no tolerance for her theatrics, no interest in trying to understand what had set her off. I simply wanted to go home, drive my daughter to her event, then spend the rest of the day vegetating. Clueless that Kelly wasn't happy with me—and hadn't been for quite some time—I brushed off her outburst with a disgusted look, then shuffled off to the car without a backward glance.

Big mistake.

The bickering went on through the rest of the day, and continued into Sunday. That night, Kelly blew sky high. "If I didn't have kids, I'd separate from you," she said forcefully. "I'd move out. I can't live inside your energy anymore. It's too big. I'm exhausted."

Man, was she heated. *This*, over a minor attempt to get her ass in gear and moving? I'd never seen her like this before. She was being so damned theatrical. Over the subsequent months and years, I would learn just how unhappy she was – not just with me and our marriage, but with her whole life. But I was way too defended to see any of that at that moment in time.

The next morning as I boarded a plane back to Portsmouth, things still weren't right between us. Kelly had retreated a million emotional miles away and wasn't talking to me. Her behavior confused and scared me. Yet I felt no sense of urgency. Whatever this was about, I knew the tension would pass; it always did. Whatever discomfort and panic I felt, I knew it was short term and would pass. If I only knew at that moment how naïve my thinking was.

In hindsight, of course, I can see that my initial reaction to her expression of misery was more than a bit dense. But at the time it made sense to me, given the contours of our life together. Not only had we just entered our 20th year of marriage; we were five months into the second and more major phase of a massive house renovation. True, our family had outgrown the house, and our 40-year-old Colonial needed shoring up. But after years of imagining, discussing and planning, Kelly and I had settled on an architectural blueprint that, in truth, was primarily about us and our future together.

Though our plans were extravagant, we had no hesitation. Kelly and I both felt we'd earned this indulgence. For almost two decades, we'd had no money issues—mortgage aside, we simply plowed everything into the kids. Kelly had always been prudent to a fault, rarely spending anything on herself. Despite the upscale town we lived in, she had no appetite for fancy cars, stylish clothing, exclusive country clubs or glamorous vacations. Neither did I. Our tastes and priorities were completely compatible. We preferred to spend our money on our kids.

Now, though, the kids were 16, almost 15, and 10. Blink, and they'd be off to college; blink again, and they'd be out in the world. Soon, it would be just Kelly and me. Why not pamper ourselves a bit? What could be a more appropriate way to spend our hard-earned dollars than to erect a magnificent edifice to house our magnificent marriage?

So, after years of listening to our kids say, "Get a room," we'd decided to go one better: we would get ourselves a whole goddamn suite. No, better than that. We'd construct a private amusement park that would stoke our imaginations and keep our love life active well into our waning years together. The final blueprint was a gigantic hard-on. Huge master bedroom suite with a balcony overlooking the woods behind our house. Sitting room. Big bay windows. Gas fireplace complete with the handy-dandy remote to quickly set a mood. Huge walk-in closets. Then, there was the bathroom. Jacuzzi perfectly contoured for two. Double marbled sinks. Designer toilet, tucked out of sight. A heated floor. And the *piece de resistance,* a large custom-designed three-level shower (remember, we're a full foot apart in height) with two perpendicular adjustable shower heads and a built-in stone bench for—well, you get the idea. Oh yeah, while we were at it, we were also retrofitting the rest of the house; there *were* those kids, even if only for a few more precious years. That meant a total disruption of the house's electrical and plumbing systems, mounds of dust and debris, wires, nails and workmen everywhere.

There's good reason why renovations have a reputation for putting strains on a marriage. But we'd largely managed to escape the attendant discomforts because Phase I of the project had been the construction of a detached two-car garage, with a self-contained studio apartment above it. We'd designed this space, the "barn," to eventually house an aging parent or sick relative. For now, though, it was serving as the family's living quarters while Phase II—the conversion of the 2,700-sq.-ft. main house into a 4,400-sq.-ft. wonderment—proceeded. Since March, our two sons had been living in the barn's garage, while Kelly, Sarah and I slept in the studio above. The family was having a great time camping out in our reduced quarters; it seemed like a grand adventure.

We had a constant flow of workmen to handle the construction, but Kelly was handling the interior decorating herself. She selected every tile, every floorboard, every cabinet and cabinet knob, light fixture and appliance. Ignited by the possibilities, my once-frugal wife was letting her spendthrift demon run wild—and I was loving it. She has exquisite taste, Kelly. I couldn't wait to return home from Portsmouth each week to see her newest improvements.

In the end, we shelled out better than twice what we had originally paid for the house 12 years earlier, but it was all within our allotted budget. As thrilled as I was by the emerging results, I was even more excited by Kelly's passionate engagement in the process. For years, she'd been fumbling around, trying to find a focus for her creative energies. Through the years, she'd taken up and abandoned many pursuits, among them painting, sewing, technical and creative writing. Now, finally, she'd found a focus for her formidable artistic talents. She seemed absorbed, satisfied, even electrified, as she dealt with the architect, the builders and the tradesmen. I was happy to see her so happy; I, devoid of any design talent, was also happy to sit back and enjoy the ride.

Given all that, though the taste of the weekend's squabbling was bitter on my tongue as I boarded the plane for Portsmouth, it didn't cross my mind that Kelly and I might be in serious trouble. Hey, we were in the middle of (literally) building our future together. We'd already weathered the worst of it: the deconstruction. It's not easy to see the home you've lived in (and loved in) for 12 years reduced to beams, joists and studs. When our house was exposed in its skeletal glory, there had been a few nasty surprises. A completely shot electrical system. Pipes that needed replacing. Most unexpected, cracks in the foundation.

Little did I suspect that this would soon prove an apt albeit hackneyed metaphor for our marriage. Even less did I anticipate that our history together was about to catch up with us and repeat itself, only this time with reversed roles—and to far more devastating effect.

Though in August I regarded my marriage as an unbroken 19-year-long love affair with a woman who filled me with a sense of stability, security and joy, Kelly and I had been through a turbulent patch once before, prior to our marriage. In that instance, I'd been the one who'd done the blindsiding.

Eight months into what had been an idyllic courtship, I abruptly and completely out of nowhere told Kelly, "I can't marry you."

"Why?" she asked, stunned.

"I don't feel any lightning bolts," I said cavalierly.

Poor Kelly didn't know what had hit her. Up to that point, we had never discussed marriage, but we were definitely on the kind of track that tended to end at the altar. Beyond becoming lovers, we'd become best friends, which in Kelly's case, was a particularly notable achievement. While I, (a boy sandwiched between two sisters), had always had comfortable friendships with women, Kelly (the middle of three sisters) was not given to easy friendships with the opposite sex. For her, putting her trust in me was a big deal. It required conscious effort. And she'd succeeded. From the start of our relationship, she worked hard to drop what she called her "walls." She often talked about how badly she'd handled relationships with men, both romantic and otherwise, prior to meeting me. Her defenses had been high and often she'd been hurt, frequently by her own doing. Determined not to repeat those mistakes with me, she was committed to complete openness.

As a result, she shared a lot of things with me those first few months, thoughts that she hadn't shared with others. One of the topics she returned to time and again was religion. Frustrated by her Christian upbringing, she was on a personal quest to open a more direct line of communication to God, one that involved neither guilt nor intermediaries. Judaism, she'd discovered, had no middle men. She liked the idea of engaging in spiritual conversation without having to go through ministers and church authorities.

She loved the Judaic concept that if you had something to atone for, you took it directly to the Big Guy. By the time we started dating, she was already well-read on the subject of Judaism—certainly better read than I, who had done virtually no reading beyond what had been foist on me while growing up, most of it surrounding the preparation for my bar mitzvah at age 13.

Now, as I spoke vaguely of "lightning bolts," Kelly's eyes clouded with bewilderment. Did I know what I was doing? she asked. Didn't I know that lightning bolts were the stuff of fantasy, found only in story books? Was I absolutely sure of what I was saying?

"Yes," I answered.

As we parted ways, she distraught, I determined, I thought, "It is said. It is done."

Or was it?

In the coming days, I was so insensitive, so clueless that I'd squashed her like a bug, that I felt no hesitation about picking up the phone and calling her. What was the big deal? She was my best friend; of course we would continue with that aspect of our relationship.

Amazingly, Kelly continued to talk to me, painful though it must have been for her. And the more we talked, the more I couldn't shake the feeling that I had made a terrible mistake. *Lightning bolts?* What kind of horseshit excuse was that? No, the reason was something deeper and more profound, something that I could feel buzzing around the edges of my consciousness, yet couldn't pin down. I knew I missed Kelly. Was I missing something else, as well?

I got my answer two months later when I caught an early matinee of *The Chosen,* based on Chaim Potok's bestselling novel. I had long since read and forgotten this tale about a brilliant teenager named Danny Saunders, who, as the son of a revered Hasidic chief rabbi, is respected by his Hasidic elders, and regarded as his father's heir apparent. The story follows Danny's adolescent struggle with the constricting demands of Hasidic life, his doubts about his pre-ordained role as his stern father's successor, his conflicted desires for a more secular life. Along the way, he looks deep within himself to understand what is really important to him and wrestles with his certainty of an unwanted outcome: if he rejects his father's ways, it will also mean excommunication from the family he loves. In the end, he rejects his strict heritage, cuts off his *pais* (side curls), sheds his traditional black attire, and joins the less rigid Orthodox community. Judaism will remain a cornerstone of his life, but it will no longer be the keystone.

Boy, talk about a wake-up call. As I watched, initially in stunned silence, then with tears running down my face, sirens wailed in my ears. What had I done? And why? The movie gave me my answer.

While growing up beneath my parents' roof, I'd always been the dutiful son. No, that's putting it too kindly. If you're familiar with the Passover story, you may remember the story of the four sons. Remember the one who "wits not to ask"? *That* was me. Always the one to follow the rules, give my parents (especially my mother) what they expected, never question or push back. It made for a happy and safe life, relatively free of conflict. And it gave me standing as Mom's chosen one. I don't mean I was her favorite. My parents were admirably even-handed; they never played favorites or played their kids against each other. We all got our fair share of attention and love. But I was the one blessed with that extra heaping of praise—you know, for towing the line? My siblings hardly envied me; to the contrary, they expressed gratitude for my willingness to absorb that extra bit of attention from my mother and attend to her needs.

Among the regular mantras of our youth (no drugs, no motorcycles, and additionally for my sisters, no hitchhiking), the most recurrent was: "And some day, you'll marry someone Jewish."

Incredible as I find it looking back, the truth is that, though well into my 20s, it had never once occurred to me that I might marry someone outside the Jewish faith. My mother could never consider such a thing, so neither had I.

Or could I?

As the lights came up after that showing of *The Chosen*, my mind churned with thoughts I'd never before considered. Sure, I felt—and feel—a strong connection with my Jewish heritage. My father had no religious upbringing. As a young boy in Brooklyn, he'd had his nose busted for the mere offense of being a Jew. And my mother had been raised among the modern Orthodox in Miami Beach, observing all the rules and strictures up to and through college. After they married, my parents carved a hybrid, not always consistent, course. In our home, Jewish observance proved a mishmash of Reform and Conservative practices, with the occasional dose of Orthodox guilt thrown in. We were diligent about showing up for High Holiday services at the temple du jour, lighting Hanukkah candles, attending my mother's exquisite Seders. But synagogues came and went, as did infrequent religious training and Sabbath candles. While my two older siblings had to attend Hebrew school, my younger sister and I did not. Both my brother and I were bar mitzvahed, but Alan was put through grinding Orthodox training by our grandfather; I got off with Conservative Lite. None of it made much sense. We were, for instance, kosher at home to accommodate infrequent visits by my mother's relatives; unkosher away from home. The hodgepodge religious upbringing left none of my siblings with an inclination to join a congregation or rear an observant family. Only I, the dutiful son, took it as a given that I would someday do both.

By the time I left the movie theater, it was clear to me that I had dumped Kelly because she wasn't Jewish. But so fucking what? My parents had carved *their* own path. Why wasn't I carving *mine*? As soon as I hit the street, I called Kelly. "Lightning bolts, my ass," I babbled. "That was just a smokescreen. You're not Jewish, and I had refused to see it. *That's* the issue that sent me packing. Please come watch the movie with me. It explains so much that I can't put into words. I don't quite understand it all yet. But it opened a door that makes me see clearly that I *do* love you, and that I've tried to bury that love for all the wrong reasons. Please come watch the movie with me. *Please.*" She acquiesced, though with great reservation.

We caught a showing the next afternoon. Then we went for a long walk on Compo Beach. It was a cold and windy fall afternoon. The beach was empty save for one very happy golden retriever playing fetch with his owner off the nearby jetty. I spoke passionately and cried openly. I had made a huge mistake. I wanted her to forgive me. I wanted her to take me back and head down the path that explored the possibility of marriage.

Kelly ruined a new pair of shoes on that walk. Hesitantly, she agreed to try again. Yes, she said, she could forgive me. Yes, she said, she could love me. But could she ever trust me again?

The answer, it would turn out, was no. But it would take almost 20 years of marriage before my fog of assumptions and wishes—hers, too—lifted sufficiently for either of us to see that.

Meanwhile, the blessings accrued. In year three of our marriage, Mike, our athletic child, was born. Alex and his musical talents followed less than two years later. Almost five years after that came Sarah, our creative and beautiful only daughter. This small circle of life that Kelly and I had created gave me a feeling of pure exultant harmony. This was *my* family. With it, I was complete. Life was mostly lovely. And when it wasn't, Kelly and I each found ways to step around our doubts and reassure ourselves.

For me, that meant looking past the fact that after Kelly agreed to take me back all those years ago, things between us never quite returned to "normal." To be specific, our sex life took a hammering. Though we never stopped touching, hugging and kissing, she never came back in an intimate, passionate way. Making love with me, it seemed, was mostly a chore. I hungered for her, but I accepted my punishment without complaint. I even told myself I was all right with our non-sexual state of affairs. It seemed logical; I'd hurt her and now she was doing the straight-arming. Fair was fair. By signing on to that simplistic explanation, I didn't have to address the sex/sexuality problem in our marriage, and neither did she. Besides, we were so content and compatible in all other aspects of our life together. The romance and affection were still there–at least in public. Surely, so was the potential for full forgiveness. If I kept my head in the sand and didn't pick at our physical disconnect, she'd eventually come around, wouldn't she?

But she never did.

Looking back, I realize how frustrated I was literally all the time. Yet I wouldn't allow myself to see it, let alone tell anyone about our physical estrangement. I'd created this story in my head: She was my wife; we were happily married; I loved her so deeply and passionately that it was inconceivable she didn't feel the same way. I sold myself on—no, I banked my very life on—that story, and never questioned it. Why would I? Like I said: we were perfect together.

So, it's probably no surprise that I didn't take her warning shot that warm August morning very seriously. We'd weathered shit before; we'd weather this.

From Portsmouth, I called home several times daily. It was a habit we'd established early in our marriage when I'd done a lot of regional traveling as a salesman for IBM. After I joined a start-up software company in 1990 and my travels took me away for weeks at a time, sometimes to places as far off as Asia and Australia, that phone link became even more crucial to my sense of well-being.

Despite my choice of career or maybe more accurately, despite the career I stumbled into, there was nothing I hated more than being alone. When I was away from my wife, my kids, my home, I counted on the sound of Kelly's voice to alleviate the loneliness I always felt. It gave me a sense of serenity and security; it reassured me that all was good in my world.

But that week, all was *not* good in my world. Conversations home were not reassuring. Repeatedly, Kelly told me in her most acerbic tone that her rope had frayed and that she was clinging to a single strand. She said she meant business; she wanted "separation." Didn't I get that?

No. I didn't.

When I returned home that weekend, she told me she was tired of my anger. She needed rest. She couldn't handle my energy. She was scared of me. That was a new one – but one that would come back months later to haunt me. Again she dwelled on the phrase that was fast-becoming her mantra: "I want separation." *Now* did I get it?

Maybe it was her vague choice of wording: she wanted "separation," not "*a* separation." Or maybe I was too distracted by work. Or maybe I was simply an idiot. But, no, I still didn't get it.

The following Monday, I again left an angry wife behind when I boarded the plane for New Hampshire. During the 50-minute puddle jump, I wondered what the hell had blown up Kelly's ass. This fight was dragging on *way* too long. A day or two, okay. But a *full* week of this? Over a petty, churlish comment? When was she going to give it a rest?

The remainder of that work week, I had little opportunity to dwell on my domestic troubles. Problems that had been percolating at work for three months inconveniently chose this moment to explode. Since May, I'd been managing the merger of a recently-acquired software concern with the company I worked for. Both the parent company and the acquired concern were located in Portsmouth, which meant that for the first time since joining this company I was spending a lot of time at corporate headquarters, a circumstance I hardly relished. I'd taken a gamble on this company as a start-up largely to step free of IBM management jobs that had mired me in office gamesmanship. Now, after 12 years of working from a virtual office, I was once again wallowing in corporate crap.

And the cesspool was deep. In a nutshell, I'd been assigned by the president to general manage this particular transition, with instructions to teach a new corporate executive who would now be my boss about revenue generation. (Translation: Sales.) The only problem was that the guy was convinced he already had all the answers, though he came to no staff meetings, no strategy sessions, no development scheduling or support planning. I, who am very good at building consensus within a team, but very bad at sucking up to corporate VIPs, trained my energies on keeping morale high within the transitioning team. When I felt this exec got in the way of the team members and their invaluable expertise, I was not hesitant about speaking my piece.

Okay, let me rephrase that. I found it hard to keep my big mouth shut. But this team was spectacular: bright, flexible, creative. The executive, by contrast, was self-important, self-righteous and totally out of touch with reality. In the end, though, the boss always wins. I got shot.

I wasn't fired. Instead, I was sent home to sell the product of this acquired business. Instantly, the steady flow of commissions and bonuses that I'd built up over a dozen years evaporated. Once again, I'd be living on salary until I could produce a new commission stream. In effect, my income had been whacked by more than half. My ego had been whacked even harder.

I didn't feel panicked, at least not yet. But I was in a state of dazed confusion. Nothing was right—and that was wrong. I felt completely unbalanced. The refrain that kept running through my head was, "I must be dreaming." It was like someone had stuck my head in a toilet bowl and flushed; this was the stage where everything was swirling around and around much too quickly to comprehend anything. No question about it, I was in the swirly of all swirlies.

That Thursday evening, I dragged my weary carcass back home. I wasn't worried about telling Kelly what had happened. When work crises had emerged in the past, she'd always provided support and understanding; surely, she would do the same this time. Hey, my dulled brain thought, maybe this is even a blessing in disguise. Nothing like a dose of reality to put a stop to her ridiculous "I need separation" lunacy, and pull us back together.

Was my head completely lodged in that orifice where the sun doesn't shine?

Kelly expressed sympathy. "It's okay, Jonathan, you'll work it out." But neither my work problems nor our changed financial situation stilled her mantra. In coming days, she trotted it out again and again, elaborating on her theme. "I don't need you anymore. You're way too needy. What I need is separation. Don't you get it?" Her tone of voice just got uglier and uglier. There was no gentleness, no kindness, no sense of love or compassion in it. Who was this woman? And why was she being such a bitch?

Though I remember few other specifics about that weekend, one conversation remains clearly etched in my mind. Kelly and I were standing in the driveway that Sunday afternoon having another very unfulfilling discussion when two maniacs came vroom-vrooming up our driveway on motorcycles. Who were these idiots making all that noise and polluting the environment? When they took off their helmets, I was startled to see that one of them was my buddy, Russ.

Russ Reed and his wife Mary Ellen live down the street from Kelly and me. A fun-loving, high-energy, New Age couple, the Reeds are our closest and most trusted friends in Doylestown. I adore Mary Ellen; I worship Russ. He has an infectious, joyous approach to life that I only wish I could emulate. Despite an earlier failed marriage, several financial reversals and a lot of other cow dung along the way, the guy always manages to emerge out the other end of the dark tunnel with a fresh perspective and a sense of renewal. Twelve years my senior, he loves life way too much to waste time on negativity.

Anyway, when Russ took off his helmet, all I remember seeing were his eyes. They were so wide and wild with excitement that it would have been easy to think he was in a drug-induced state. But no, the only narcotic was the motorcycle, Russ's new toy. "We just rode to the beach!" he roared with elation, as Kelly migrated over to talk to his nephew and riding partner, Boo.

"You mean the Jersey shore?" I said skeptically. "It's an hour and a half away."

"Yep. My first time on a highway, and it was awesome. Boo's been giving me pointers and helping me get comfortable with the bike. I'm exhausted from the roundtrip, but it was amazing. Jonathan, you *have* to take the DOT motorcycle safety course *immediately* so I have someone to ride with next summer. Boo's going home and I'll have no one to ride with."

"But I'm not allowed to ride motorcycles," I replied.

That was a conversation stopper. For a long moment, Russ and I just stared at each other. Finally, I said with a sheepish grin, "I didn't really say that, did I?"

"Uh, *yeah* ...What's *that* all about?" He shot me a big smile, and after another pause, we both cracked up.

"I'm 46 years old," I said, shaking my head in amused disbelief. "Can you believe I would say something so ridiculous? Growing up, my mother exacted only two promises from my brother and me: no drugs, no motorcycles. It's never occurred to me that I *could* ride one. I've never even thought to think it through. I mean, Mom had spoken, right? The dutiful son lives on! Man, I have *got* to grow up."

"Well give it up, dude. You *have* to do this with me. It's too damn much fun to do alone."

Though I nodded, at that moment the idea of doing something simply for the pleasure of it, something for me and nobody else, something life-affirming and playful and just because I wanted to, not because someone said I had to or wasn't allowed to, was a lot like the idea of Kelly and me separating: Not a possibility. Not on my radar screen. In a word, unthinkable.

2. THE TAI CHI MASTER
V. THE BOXER

"If only I had…"

Over the next two years, I would pose that hypothetical a million times. Mostly, I would wonder how I could have better handled Kelly's initial withdrawal. If only I had listened, and not blamed, whined or begged. If only I had looked harder at myself instead of taking aim at her. If only I had asked myself, "What's so great about *me* that Kelly should still be in love with me?" If only I had asked, Am I loving enough? Am I understanding, supportive, open, sensitive to her feelings? Am I caring, compassionate, a good conversationalist, a better listener? Am I entertaining and interesting, enthusiastic and inspiring? Am I romantic in a way that suits her needs? Thoughtful? Considerate? Most of all, am I a good friend to her?

It would take me a lot longer to turn some of those questions back on myself. Am I getting what *I* need from this relationship? What do *I* get to be in this relationship? What have *I* given up to stay in this marriage? Is it worth the price? What do I want?

At the outset, though, I was incapable of considering any of it. During those first few months of what Kelly kept calling her "disconnect"—what I would quickly come to regard as her damned abandonment—I just kept telling myself, "This is a temporary thing." Okay, so she's not happy with me. Okay, so she's bent out of shape and this fight is lasting longer than usual. Okay, so my angry responses and hostile silences aren't exactly helping us to confront whatever shit she's stepped in. *This will pass. She'll come around. We'll get through it.* I still didn't take her talk of "separation" seriously. I figured she was just pissed. It was annoying, frustrating, and inconsiderate of her to keep harping on my failures as a husband, yes, but, hey, she'd snap out of it. She always did.

By October, we were in therapy, both jointly and individually. Mind you, I saw no need for therapy. To me, therapy was for the sort of whack jobs depicted in movies like *One Flew Over the Cuckoo's Nest.* That's what my parents had told me and my siblings repeatedly and pointedly about mental health care. So that was my fixed and inflexible opinion. But I wasn't a complete idiot. If this was what Kelly thought would make things right between us, then I'd walk the walk, and talk the psychobabble talk.

I kind of had to. She had gone back to school and a year earlier, had earned a masters degree in Psychology – Counseling; since then, she'd started practicing, with a specialty in domestic violence. Psychology was her world now, and I truly wanted to support her new career; it made her so happy. Yet as I listened to her in the therapist's office, I was deaf to her pain and dissatisfaction. *Her* pain. *Her* dissatisfaction. That's the way I regarded it. Distant and unconnected to me. A byproduct of her new degree.

Mostly, I tried to apply the tai chi tactic of using my opponent's strength against her. Every time Kelly would come at me, I'd turn it around and push it right back at her. "My god," I'd say, "aren't you over this *yet?* Can't you see how much I *love* you? Get over it already." Then, I'd roll my eyes in disgust, ooze superiority, walk away. If I was feeling particularly tolerant, I'd absorb her endless talk, nod my head sagely and say, "I hear you" or "Uh-huh," just to show I was listening. Then, I'd summarize and, drawing on my get-the-job-done expertise, offer a solution. Quick, easy … are we done yet? How typically male.

When these tricks failed, I resorted to indifference. After all, there wasn't really a *problem*; this wasn't really *happening*. If I just kept my head down and ignored her persistent talk of unhappiness, this would all go away. You know, step around—not through—the pile of shit? That was a strategy that had always worked for me in the past. I banked on it now as I refused to engage with her, telling myself, "She's just in a funk. It's a stage she's going through. Maybe she's having an extra long period or is entering menopause."

When I exhausted agitation, anger and blame, I tried self-righteous martyrdom. "How can you act like this?" "Why are you doing this to me?" "How can you treat me like this when you know how much I love you?"

Finally, I reached into my emotional arsenal and trotted out the deadliest weapon of all: guilt. "Can't you see the pain you're causing me?" "Can't you see what you're doing to the *kids*?" In my very Jewish experience, this was the one I knew I could count on to bring her to her knees. Anytime now, she'd be groveling with contrition and saying, "I was wrong. I see the error of my ways. I love you so much. How could I possibly have thought otherwise? What *was* I thinking? Please, forgive me. And now, please rip off my clothes and ravish my body so I can show you how wrong I've been." Make up sex can be so great!

Strange thing is, it never quite worked out that way. Instead, at Halloween, Kelly reached into her own arsenal and extracted a weapon that delivered a precise blow that gave new meaning to the holiday greeting, "Trick or Treat."

John Volpe, my longtime best friend, had stopped in for dinner. It was a rare treat for me. John lives way out on the north fork of Long Island, at least four hours away, so we don't get to spend much time together.

John had been my first big customer back in 1980 when I was a rookie salesman at IBM. At the time, he was the new Director of Information Technology for a large manufacturing concern, hired to handle the company's conversion of their mainframe computer systems from Univac to IBM. In the process of winning and installing the business, John and I became buddies. During that period, John's first marriage, a union of more than 20 years, began to unravel. He had five sons and a wife who'd recently gone back to school to get her master's degree in counseling. Like Kelly would do many years later, John's wife woke up one morning and announced that she was no longer happy in her marriage and no longer in love with her husband. She made it clear to John that he had to make some wholesale changes; she put the burden on him to rescue a marriage he hadn't thought was in trouble. It ended quickly and painfully in a divorce John never saw coming, the poor bastard.

Around that same time, I met Kelly, who'd recently transferred from one of IBM's New York City offices to my branch in Norwalk, Conn., to serve as our large systems office automation specialist. As part of my ongoing sales effort, I dutifully dragged her off to meet John and my other large customers. In other words, John met Kelly right around the same time I did.

When I started dating Kelly a year later, John was deep in the throes of his divorce. By then, John and Kelly had become business pals. While Kelly and I courted, she and John also became close personal friends. As the years passed, he was always a part of our major occasions, and we were a part of his. He attended our wedding. When each of our kids was born, Kelly and I asked him to be godfather, an affirmation of the love and trust we each felt for him. And when he remarried, Kelly and I were there to watch him and Linda exchange vows.

Though John and I talked by phone and emailed each other frequently, I hadn't seen him in many months. So, it was great to have an evening together. More than ever, I needed his friendship and counsel. He arrived at our house sensitive to the disconnect Kelly was going through. It wasn't only that I'd shared details of our troubles when we talked by phone. Three or four years earlier when Kelly had first gone back to school to earn her counseling degree, he'd warned me, from hard-won experience, that Kelly's pursuit of her masters could prove rough on me. I'd responded that I wasn't worried; our marriage was solid. He'd countered, again from experience, that a little knowledge could be brutal on a marriage; that the first person a newly-minted therapist trains her deep new insights on is her spouse. He'd also cautioned that she might "self-therapize" and retreat into a world foreign and unknown to an unsuspecting recipient—in this case, me. I didn't buy a word of it.

Here's how I learned just how right he was. John and I were in the kitchen, talking and enjoying cocktails, while I cooked dinner. When I say kitchen, I mean our new one, which after eight long months of renovation, was finally complete. In early October, we'd moved from the barn back into the main house, and it was so cool having this incredible new kitchen to play in. Kelly was out running errands. Mike, 16 at the time, was at a work station just off the kitchen, joining our conversation on and off as he chatted on his cell phone and i.m.'ed his friends. (It always amazes me how teenagers can remain connected to the people they love while they multitask.)

As John and I talked, Mike's cell phone rang. I heard him say, "Hello? Hello?" but apparently he was getting no response. After a few moments, he called to me, "Dad, this is so bizarre. It's Mom on the phone, but she doesn't know she's dialed me. She's talking to somebody in what sounds like a public place."

He handed me the phone and I put it to my ear. The background sounds were immediately identifiable: a bar or restaurant of some sort. Her voice was also unmistakable. She was talking with some guy, having what sounded like an informal conversation. She had probably been fingering the cell phone in her pocket and inadvertently hit the "call" key; I assume Mike had been the last person she'd called, so it had been his number that got redialed. It was clear she had no idea we were connected. After listening for a moment to make sure nothing was wrong, I rang off and handed the phone back to Mike, making light of Mom's clumsy mistake. Then, I returned to talking and cooking with John, and didn't give it another thought.

A little while later the house phone rang. It was Kelly, calling to say she was on her way home. "Where've you been?" I asked.

"Oh, just out running some errands," she responded vaguely.

"Where have you been?" I said again. Though I'd consciously registered nothing as wrong or amiss when I'd listened in on the earlier call, I guess something was nagging at the edges of my mind.

"What do you mean? I've been running errands," she again responded.

"Kelly, what aren't you telling me?" I heard myself say more sharply. "Who were you with?" I wasn't angry, just annoyed that she didn't appear to be telling a complete story.

Abruptly, she blurted, "Jonathan, we need to talk. We need to talk *now*. I'll be home in a second. I'm less than a mile from the house." Then, she hung up.

Weird, I thought. Something was definitely wrong. When I repeated the conversation to John, he gave me a look of sympathy that I wouldn't understand for a few minutes, but won't forget until the day I die.

I excused myself and walked outside to meet Kelly. The next few seconds would change my life forever. The recurring memory of it may well haunt me for many lifetimes to come.

Kelly roared up the driveway at a frantic pace, pushing our Volvo wagon well beyond the revs where the gear should have been changed. She pulled in front of the garage, braked hard and parked at an awkward angle, something I'd never seen her do before. She looked panicked. Still, nothing registered in my mind as unusual. Was she not feeling well? When she neither moved from her seat nor turned off the engine, I opened the front passenger door and got in. Her eyes were wide with something I couldn't read. Alarm? Distress? Fear?

"I've been seeing Scott and I think I'm in love with him," she blurted, without preamble.

Say, what? "Huh?"

"I've been seeing Scott since early summer and I think I'm in love with him."

"Who's 'Scott'?"

"Scott. The electrician."

What? Did I hear that right? The *electrician?* The one tradesman still working in our house? You're having an affair? An *affair?* With the fucking electrician???

In that nanosecond, my whole world turned upside down. Instantly, everything started to spin. I couldn't catch my breath. I began to hyperventilate. Kelly was talking, but I wasn't hearing. There was an ocean crashing in my head and a pain exploding in my stomach. The car was swirling uncontrollably through a universe that I didn't recognize. Everything was blurry and moving too fast; I wasn't keeping up. My wife was telling me something, something that was fast-erasing my reality, something that promised my life would never again be the same.

And Kelly knew it. She knew that infidelity was the one fear that could sink me. I'd told her exactly that when we'd first started dating, long before we'd even gotten serious. If you ever really want to hurt me, I'd told her, cheat on me. I'm a lot of things, both good and bad. But I'm always, always faithful. I'm the living stereotype of the nice Jewish boy—good husband, good father, good provider…monogamous to a fault. That is supposed to cut both ways. You want to eviscerate me, take my guts and serve them up on a platter? Cheat on me.

Now, without warning, she'd upended my entire existence and unceremoniously dumped me in hell. Where in the script of my life had I signed up for *this*? Was she kidding? Was she fucking joking??

Through the blur, I heard snippets of what was tumbling out of her mouth. "We just go out for coffee a lot …Eighty percent of what we talk about is his wife and his pending divorce that she doesn't want …I haven't told you because I didn't think you would understand…We're not sleeping together but we love each other …I was going to tell you soon because I haven't been able to stand the betrayal …"

"I need to pick up Alex at rehearsal," I stammered. That was all I could muster. I went into the kitchen, mumbled something to John about being right back, then got in my car and fled.

I have little recollection of the next six weeks or so. What I do know is that a mind-crushing depression moved in fast and furiously. It grabbed hold of my mind and body, and would not let go. It took away my appetite. It took away my ability to sleep. It took away my ability to think lucidly. To say I was in a daze would be a gross understatement. I couldn't speak. I couldn't work. I couldn't function. Every breath was painful and laborious. I was in complete meltdown mode. This was a place I'd never been before—not even close—and it scared the bejesus out of me. It also scared my poor kids. They watched their confident father come apart at the seams, then show no indication he would be able to pull himself back together. It was all I could do to hold my head up and make conversation with them. I'm not sure I was able to do even that much.

I had no idea it was possible to fall so far, so fast. Until this moment, my life had been so steady, so easy. But with one atomic blast, Kelly had unleashed my violent furies—demons I didn't even know existed—from some hidden compartment buried deep inside me. Now, they came roaring to the surface. My fear of abandonment. My fear of betrayal. My fear of rejection. My fear of not being loved. My fear of being lonely. And the biggest of them all— my fear of being alone.

During these weeks, conversations with Kelly were brutal and one-sided. I was like a punch drunk boxer taking a battering from a far more skilled opponent. I just stood there and absorbed hit after hit, waiting for the next one to land.

Upper cut: "I need separation. Don't you get it?"

Cross punch: "I can stand on my own two feet and live just fine without you. You need to do the same. You're too needy. I used to be that way. And if we find each other again as two independent, strong people, so be it."

Right jab: "You should go away for six months and find yourself. Maybe do the Peace Corps or Habitat for Humanity. You need to learn to be your own strong person."

Left jab: "I've felt used my whole life. I've never really been in love with anybody until this."

Double-fisted combination: "Don't you get it? Scott was just a catalyst. He was meant to come into my life to wake me up. It was cosmically contracted. We never slept together. It was just the emotional awakening that was so necessary. It's so necessary for you too."

Right cross: "You're just like my father. You take care of all of my needs and our family's needs. But you want me to be a certain way. You have this box you want me in to fit your definition of a wife."

Left cross: "You don't really know who I am. We never stay up all night talking."

Haymaker: "I married you because I needed rescuing. I was desperate. You saved my life. Now I don't need saving. I need to be me. I don't feel like I can be me around you anymore."

Knock-out punch: "I don't need you anymore."

When I'd come to, I'd beg, entreat, plead. When Kelly wouldn't respond, I'd sink deeper into confusion and misery. I missed my wife. *Desperately.*

Meanwhile, my furies grew louder and louder, while my daily reality grew murkier and murkier. What was this ugly, terrifying monster that had seized control of my mind? I thought I was going insane. Really.

During these weeks, the pain literally took me to my knees. Once down, I lacked the resources to get back up for hours on end. All I could grasp was that I'd been decked by the woman I love. Far worse, Kelly seemed apologetic only that she hadn't told me sooner. Otherwise, her posture was smug and all-knowing. She wanted what she wanted—now. My designated role, it appeared, was to stand by calmly as she destroyed everything I held dearest. Her arrogance was appalling. My willingness to accept it if she'd only come back to me was pathetic. But it would take more than two years before I could see it that way.

This was more pain than I'd suspected was humanly possible. I thought it was more than I could handle. At times, I thought I *couldn't* handle it. I thought about *not* handling it. Ever been there? Ever contemplated it? I hadn't until now. The possibility scared the daylights out of me. I had three kids. I *had* to handle it. But ohgodohgohgodohgod, how was I going to get through this? Why wasn't I handling this *better*? Why was I imploding? Why wasn't I keeping this in *perspective*? What the hell was *wrong* with me?

A year and a half later, I would describe to a new therapist how humiliated I felt by my collapse. He would respond with an observation as startling and poignant as it was simple: "Jonathan, you told me that you never had trauma of any sort in your life up until that point. You told me what a blessed life you led for your first 46 years. What makes you think you even remotely had the tools to handle a crisis of such magnitude?"

Man, did he ever come along 18 months too late. During the worst of my meltdown, it would have helped to know that I was *entitled* to feel flattened and out of control; that my feelings were understandable; that my reaction was normal, maybe even inevitable. It would have made my disintegration more acceptable to me. At the least, it would have taken the humiliation and shame out of it.

Or so I tell myself now. More likely, I wouldn't have heard the guy at all. Why? Because during those initial weeks of seeming collapse, I was actually only reeling; it would be months yet before I would begin to understand that I was going down for the count. I didn't yet grasp the dimensions of the catastrophe that had just befallen me, my marriage, my life. The only thing I grasped was that Kelly, the mother of my children, the woman I unquestioningly assumed I would spend the rest of my life with, had just given me a hard shove, and I was in a free fall that seemed to have no bottom.

3. LITTLE J

What do you mean there's another man? How could you do this to me? I'm not man enough for you? What have I done that makes you want to hurt me so much? How could you do this to me? Have you thought about the kids? Our family? Have you even considered the long-term ramifications? The fucking electrician...who's still working in my house, still taking my money? How could you do this to me?

My head noise was loud, persistent and unbearable. With my one true confidante now my torturer, I turned to the only person I thought would be understanding: my therapist. Overnight I went from skeptic to frantic believer. I'm glad I did. Not only did I want to be in therapy, I needed to be there.

One look and Janet grasped that I'd learned about Kelly and the electrician. She already knew about their relationship. Apparently she and Kelly had discussed the affair frequently in Kelly's individual sessions. "Why didn't you tell me?" I demanded.

"It wasn't my place to tell you or not tell you," she answered. "Kelly had to do that. We worked for a long time on why she felt she couldn't tell you and how she would ultimately do that."

"I feel like I've been lied to," I countered. "I feel like a sucker, the last one to know. I feel humiliated, confused, scared and a thousand other emotions that I can't begin to describe, none of them good. I want my wife back. I want my life back."

"Jonathan, she didn't *have* an affair. Don't you get that?"

"No, not even close!" I roared. "How can you tell me she didn't sleep with him? She's been seeing this guy for over six months behind my back. She talks all starry-eyed about being hit with a thunderbolt – and this all these years after telling me how the lightning bolt effect is something only found in story books. 'It just happened,' she moans. 'There he was across the driveway one morning'." My mimicry of her was vitriolic.

"Let me rephrase it then: she didn't have a *physical* affair. She never slept with him. Believe it. What I find so interesting is that they spent most of their time discussing his wife and failing marriage. I need to repeat this: there *was no physical affair.*"

"Yeah, right," I replied acidly. "Why should I believe her? Hasn't Kelly been telling me how in love she is with this blue collar asshole?" I was so angry that I was spitting and sinking to juvenile name-calling. My ego, god my ego... really hurt.

Poor Janet. I argued, ranted and raved. I cried uncontrollably. She remained calm and professional. In the end, she conceded that emotional betrayal can be as bad, or worse, than physical betrayal. What she wanted me to understand was that my marriage was in deep crisis. She stressed that Kelly's "stepping out" was neither unusual nor uncommon; when people are unhappy and confused and they can't articulate it, they act out. Kelly, she said, was lost and didn't know how to proceed. Scott was just a catalyst to open her up to herself. *He wasn't the issue.*

Yeah, right. At that moment, my jealousy was intense—and it would rage for many months to come. How could I ever forgive Kelly for such a betrayal? She'd hit me in the place we both knew was my most vulnerable spot.

Janet's next point was very clear: If a *real* relationship was going to evolve between Kelly and me, it was absolutely necessary for me to move past my fear. Forgiveness was essential. This was no simple process, she warned. It would take courage, endurance and an open mind. I had to be willing to look at myself.

"Why me?" I shot back. "*She's* the one who's acting out. *She's* the one who betrayed our marriage and everything that's sacred. *She's* the one…"

"Hold it right there," Janet snapped. "Do you really think this is only about *her*? Do you really think you had no role in this crisis? Do you really think that you are without blame here? Do you think your marriage is in jeopardy only because of her? Wake up, Jonathan." Her stare was powerful and penetrating, and her intensity took me by surprise. I had never seen her like this before.

"But I didn't do anything. *She* did."

I was crying hard again. I cried a lot during that session. I cried a lot throughout my ensuing depression. I cried for damn near two years.

"Jonathan, listen to me. Kelly's supposed affair was not caused by love. It was motivated by any number of complex issues that are raging uncontrollably inside her, none of which she understands right now. What she thought was a godsend and a sudden release from jail has caused her more pain and confusion in the end. She has to come to grips with herself now, what she really feels and what she really wants. She will need to climb inside herself to find the answers. Only *she* can do that. That's why she is asking for separation; there is nothing you can do to solve her issues. You are only in the way. She is scared of you, your anger, your reactions. She is scared of herself and what she might find when she digs deep enough. What you *can* do right now is work on yourself. You have to face your own demons before you can even think about rebuilding your marriage."

"Let me guess. You're going to tell me, '*Only I can make me happy*'."

"Actually, you're right," she shot back. "Kelly can't make you happy. Nobody can make you happy but yourself. So let's start looking. Are you game?"

I was pissed and unwilling to be placated. "Is that a challenge?"

"No," she replied, sounding like she had entered a trance. "Things falling apart is a kind of testing and also a kind of healing. You think that there is an easy answer. There isn't. The truth is that things don't really get solved. They come together and they fall apart. Then they come together again and they fall apart again. The healing comes from letting there be room for all of this to happen: room for grief, room for relief, room for misery, room for joy. Letting there be room for not knowing is the most important thing of all. Life is like that. We don't really know anything. We call something bad; we call it good. But really we just don't know."

Janet snapped out of her reverie and looked me hard in the eyes. "The only time we ever know what's really going on is when the rug's been pulled out from under us and we can't find anywhere to land. We use these situations either to wake ourselves up or to put ourselves to sleep. Right now, Jonathan, in this very instant of your groundlessness and pain, is the seed of taking care of yourself and discovering who you really are. The fears that are so crippling to you are only a resistance to your emotional awareness. You must confront those fears and transform them. I don't know how you've gone so long without facing this kind of pain. You've been protecting yourself your whole life, haven't you. Why?"

I looked at her dumbfounded. "I don't know."

"I don't know" had always been my favorite answer to "why" or "how do you feel" questions. It made it easy *not* to have to think or feel. It made it easy to keep things at the surface and not risk ridicule, anger or pain. It made it easy not to expose myself—even to myself. This was the beginning of the end of that protective cover.

Toward the end of the session, Janet lent me a book called *Homecoming: Reclaiming and Championing Your Inner Child* by John Bradshaw. Oddly enough, he had written the book just as he himself was getting divorced after a 20-year marriage. "Take a look at this between now and the next session," she said. "Buy yourself a copy. This is all about looking at and healing your inner child."

"You've got to be kidding," I snorted. "Inner child? What kind of psycho-mumbo-jumbo crap is that?"

"Don't judge it yet," she responded. "Bradshaw's basic premise is that when a child's development is arrested, when feelings are repressed, a person grows up to be an adult with an angry, hurt child inside. This child will spontaneously contaminate the person's adult behavior."

"That's ridiculous."

"It's proved to be powerful stuff," she countered calmly. "He says that the neglected, wounded inner child of the past is the greatest source of human misery. He says that until we reclaim and champion that inner child, he will continue to act out and contaminate our adult lives. Bradshaw has a simple technique to get at this inner child. I think it would be effective with you."

Janet then assigned me an exercise from the Bradshaw book. In a journal, I was to write a letter to my adult self from my inner child, writing with my opposite hand. (I'm right-handed, so that meant using my left.) The mere act of struggling with my untrained hand, she explained, would put me more in the mental framework of a child. After I'd written the letter, I was to respond to my inner child with a letter from my adult self. The emotional, angry, out-of-control Jonathan, she instructed, was the child within; the adult Jonathan was mature, calm, loving, protective and … well … adult.

* * *

That night, I sat alone on my bed, struggling against my resistance. By now, Kelly had taken to sleeping on the couch in the sitting room off our master bedroom, claiming that she "needed separation." Mind you, I could see the couch from our bed unless the double doors were closed. Watching her settle on the couch instead of getting into bed with me was like a hot poker to the midsection. When the doors were closed, just knowing she was on the other side hurt far, far worse. To me, that short distance seemed like cruel and unusual punishment. All I wanted to do was reach out and hold her. I was certain my pain and anger would evaporate if she would just say, "I love you, Jonathan."

But she didn't. And the pain just kept on accruing. For three months now, I'd barely slept. Work was out; nothing cerebral was functioning. I was so steeped in my misery that I couldn't even communicate coherently with my kids. At this point, I hurt so bad that I was willing to try anything—even this moronic exercise. Finally, I set pen to paper.

Holy shit. I stared dumbstruck at the letter. I had no idea how the words had gotten onto the paper. They'd been written without conscious thought. Yet there they were. Scary.

What now?

Answer the little guy, something inside me prodded. So I did.

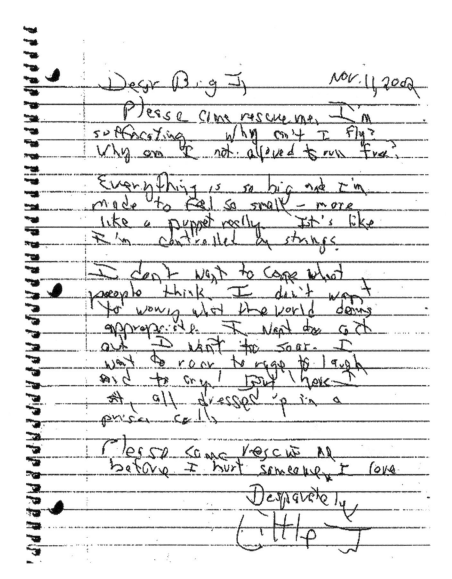

Dear Little J:

I see how scared you are. I see how panic sets in when you think about breaking free. It is very difficult. But know, sweet young J, that I am here to love you. I am here to wrap you up in my arms and protect you from the fear. I am here to take you away from the pain.

I THOUGHT WE WERE HAPPY

If you so choose, you may leave the house that binds you so tight and come live only with me. I will love you with all of my heart and support you in every way possible. I will protect you when your fears run amok. I am your friend and will love you for who you really are and who you can really be.

When you choose to fly, open the cell door and leap in to the abyss. I will be here to catch you, to support you, to love you and to nourish you.

I know you are afraid. Just think about it for a while.

Lovingly, J

Almost unconsciously, Little J wrote back:

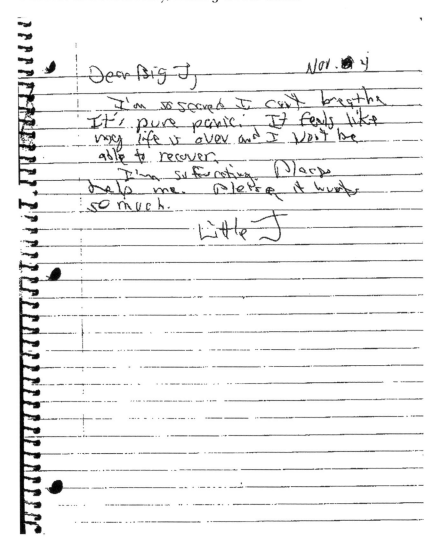

For the next three months I worked this exercise. I had to.
I—whoever—couldn't and wouldn't stop. I have notebooks full of
these letters. They are alternately funny, sad, and angry. They vent
rage, frustration and fear. They expose the loneliness and dread
of being alone that was terrorizing me. What started out as the

dumbest assignment I'd ever heard of produced an amazing self-portrait of a man-child in deep crisis. The experience helped me to start facing my real demons and issues. Once started, there was no turning back.

Kelly was pretty brutal through this period, which extended from her initial withdrawal in August, past the Halloween disclosure of her relationship with the electrician, to the end of November. Later, I would come to understand that she was struggling to come to grips with her own "stuff." But during these months (and for many months to follow), her own process was often pointed right between my eyeballs. "If we didn't have kids, I'd separate," was one oft-repeated phrase.

Another of her knife-edged favorites was, "You need to learn how to stand on your own two feet and not lean so heavily on me. I don't need you, and I don't need to lean on you anymore."

"I'm not in love with you, and I may never have been," was a favorite standby and cold slap that doubled me over each and every time.

The piece de resistance? "It's not right that I wasn't allowed to end my relationship with Scott [the electrician] on my own terms. I need closure. That you and Janet are telling me I can't see him anymore is wrong."

Wrong? Who the hell did she think she was?

Part of the answer to that question was as galling as it was obvious. A bona fide therapist with a degree to prove it, Kelly was determined to use her newly minted counseling skills on me. Now that she was an *expert*, she was bent on helping me work through my depression, my pain, my hurt, my anger. She seemed strangely oblivious to the fact that *she* was the source of my distress as she tackled my "problem" with a clinical zeal stripped of any warmth or compassion. Along with her many annoying classroom techniques, she offered an ever-growing list of books that she insisted, "You absolutely must read." One of the books she so blithely dropped on my bed was *After the Affair* by Janis Abrahms Spring. I guess this was her way of assuaging her own guilt. Like an idiot, I dutifully read it.

Basically, the book states that affairs are normal. It also acknowledges that emotional affairs often leave worse scars on the spouse than physical ones, but I suspect Kelly chose not to dwell on that point. The author, along with her husband Michael Spring, describes how couples can survive an indiscretion and rescue their marriage. On one point, they are very clear: the offending spouse *must* give up the paramour immediately and *never* see him/her again. The book clearly states that this is the cornerstone of healing a marriage in need of reconstruction.

I highlighted the appropriate passage in yellow marker, and then underlined it in red pen lest Kelly might miss the highlighting. Then I returned the book to Kelly and said, "The book *you* gave me to read because it was *so* relevant, clearly states that the betrayer must not see the person she had the affair with ever again."

"Books aren't always right," she responded with an air of serene superiority. "They just express viewpoints and opinions. I gave you the book to open your mind to the possibilities, that's all."

Beautiful. Fuckin' beautiful.

She inserted the knife deeper and began to twist. "Scott and I are such good friends. I really cherish his friendship. I don't want to lose that. It's not fair that you are making me sever the most wonderful friendship I've ever had."

Let me get this straight: My wife had been secretly spending time with another man. Now, she was asking me to sit like a good boy and be okay with it? How deep did she think the knife could go?

Please understand, I've never been one of those macho types, so overprotective and insecure that I feel a need to keep my wife from her male friends (or female, for that matter). I *wanted* Kelly to enjoy friendships with men. Why wouldn't I? I regard my life as greatly enriched by my friendships with the opposite sex; I wanted no less for Kelly. Besides, Kelly had always been honest, a woman of integrity. I trusted her completely—and never would have thought to do otherwise had she not turned her romantic attentions to another man. On this much, we both agree.

"Have I *ever* questioned your friendships?" I now asked. "Have I *ever* tried to restrict who you spend time with, who you talk to, who your friends are?" My voice rose, my anger getting the better of me, as is my way when I'm in pain.

"No, you've always been wonderful about that," she said. "You've always pushed me to pursue new friendships, irrespective of gender. In fact, I was surprised that you never minded me playing golf with Stephen those first few summers we lived here."

Stephen? Who the hell was *that?* I searched my foggy mind and landed on our lawn guy. He was a "hunk," about 15 years Kelly's junior. Until this moment, it had never occurred to me that their friendship had been anything but platonic. Now, I felt a horror rise in my throat. "Did you have an affair with him, too?"

"No. How dare you even insinuate it! I was completely faithful to you." Now *her* voice was rising and indignant. "I never cheated or lied to you in any way, at least until this. Don't you understand that the entire time I was seeing Scott, I felt guilty? It was wrong what I did, there is no excuse. But I was too scared to tell you. It ate away at me. I spent hours talking to Janet and Mary Ellen [her best friend] about the guilt and the shame of it. You and I don't communicate well, Jonathan. You never hear what I'm saying. When I want to talk about our relationship or anything that makes you uncomfortable, you get angry at me and shut me down. I'm just plain scared of you."

"But your 'guilt' and 'shame' aren't enough to make you go cold turkey with Scott?" I spat.

"I don't know what I want," she moaned. "If we were really able to communicate, I would have told you about it right from the start. If you weren't so defensive and angry, and really loved me the way you say you do, then this never would have happened."

There it was: *my* fault.

"Instead, we would have discussed it," she continued. "It would have been an academic exercise. You would have said, 'Wow, you have feelings for this guy just by looking at him from across a parking lot. Isn't that interesting. How does being hit by this lightning bolt make you feel?' and we would have discussed it. We would have looked at it from all sides. We would have laughed about it and tried to understand it. I never would have acted out had we been able to do that. Instead, your defensiveness and anger got in the way."

Wow, you have feelings for this guy? What fucking planet did she come from? Had her head always been stuck this far up her ass?

"I have felt isolated and lonely for so long. Around Scott I feel like there is nothing I can't do. I feel free and energized. Around you I only feel evaporated and overpowered."

"Gee, that's funny," I snapped. "I thought we had a great marriage."

"So did I," she said quietly. "Scott kept asking me what was wrong with my marriage. Why wasn't I happy? I kept saying to him that I was a happily married woman. I woke up one day and realized that I wasn't."

"Gee, Kelly," I commented with more than a little sarcasm. "Don't you think Scott just *might* have had a *little* personal motivation, a little self-serving agenda, in pushing that button?"

Despite my cynicism, Kelly couldn't have put it any more plainly. Yet, I still didn't believe her. Each time she demanded, "Don't you get it?" all I could think was, "No, not at all." And I truly didn't.

Absurd as it may sound, it still hadn't crossed my mind that we wouldn't be all right. Instead, I nurtured a fantasy that any minute now, my wife would jump out of the closet and yell, "April Fools!" It would take the double whammy of those most family-oriented of holidays—Thanksgiving and Christmas—to begin to put that happy delusion to rest once and for all.

4. THE HOLIDAY HORROR SHOW

Thanksgiving that year involved a Lewis get-together that had been in the planning for the better part of a year. My entire family was coming to Doylestown not only to see our newly renovated house, but also to celebrate my parents' 50th wedding anniversary. This would be the first time Kelly and I had hosted my whole family at once, and it was a large crowd: my parents, my three siblings, their spouses and children, and Gatha, who'd helped raise my siblings and me in Westport. All told, we numbered 18. Suffice it to say, I was in no condition to play host.

Coming into the long holiday weekend, my parents and siblings knew that Kelly and I were going through a rough patch. I had discussed neither my depression nor the particulars of my marital turbulence with any of them. But as I'm not very good at hiding my emotions, most of them had figured out that I was in bad shape and that the situation was grim.

Thankfully, there were no fireworks, no fights, no embarrassing spats. The incredible results of our renovation were shown off and admired. My folks' anniversary was celebrated in style. Everybody seemed to have as good a time as could be expected. Kelly put up a brave front, trying hard to make things easy for everybody. So did the members of my family, a loving clan prone to protecting their own. It couldn't have been easy for my parents, secure in their own marriage, to see me, my marriage and the home of three of their grandchildren in such a fragile state.

I was less worried what my brother and sisters might think. Born within five years of each other, the four of us come from the same generation; we can relate to each other's problems and issues. Alan, the oldest, is two years ahead of me and has always been my best friend. Unfortunately for me, he's lived in Florida for the last 24 years, so we don't get to spend nearly enough time together. Ann, known as Pooz since she was three years old, is the youngest, two years behind me. She's my emotional twin, but was living on the West coast at the time so we don't get to see each other much at all.

That leaves Jill. Just short of a year older than me, Jill lives a little over an hour's drive away in New Jersey. We get to spend time together. We even went to college together. Jill graduated Cum Laude from Princeton; I graduated Cum Difficulty. That basically sums up the difference between us. Jill is intellectual; I'm a salesman. She's incisive; I'm hail-fellow-well-met. She's always been introspective; until this upheaval, I wasn't. I adore my big sister. She rescued me when no one else understood.

Over the holiday weekend, my brother's best friend from college, who lives only a few miles from me but far enough away to take us out of suburbia and into rural America, invited us for a walk in the woods. A hike seemed just the thing to get some fresh air and help digest too much turkey. As about a dozen of us set off on our trek in sweatshirts and sneakers, the sky was blue, the air crisp, the breeze gentle. The group quickly broke into smaller clusters. I found myself jumping between the lively discussions, enjoying both the conversations and the break from my misery. At some point, I dropped to the back of the pack to talk with Jill.

This was the first occasion Jill and I had found time alone together during the weekend. One thing you can say unequivocally about my older sister, who's an accomplished author and professional journalist of 25 years: she doesn't beat around the bush. Let me rephrase that. She is blunt, honest and to the point. She doesn't mince words. With Jill you never find yourself saying, "Yes, but what do you *really* think?"

Her opening gambit was gentle and kind, with a touch of the kid glove. "You look like shit."

That's my sister. But I guess it was hard not to notice. I hadn't slept in a month, and I was down at least 10 pounds. The 10 pounds might sound like a nice by-product of the situation, but I didn't have it to lose. I've always been lean and lanky, able to eat whatever I want, whenever I want, without consequence. But 10 pounds off and I begin to look malnourished. (I started my disintegration with 184 pounds on my 6'2" frame. At the height of the depression, I would drop to 150 pounds.)

Over the next hour, I bared my soul to Jill. Other than Kelly and my therapist, I hadn't spoken to anybody about the situation. Through tears I described my agony, the pain of my wife's separation, the onset of my crushing depression, what I was learning about myself in therapy. The more I talked and sobbed, the farther back we fell from the other hikers. Throughout, Jill grilled me with questions, probing what I was experiencing. She didn't get emotional and she didn't feel it necessary to cry along with me. Instead, with her journalistic instincts, she questioned me about every aspect of the situation. Her method of talking and asking questions helped me to articulate my situation clearly. I knew my work in therapy was helping, but I hadn't been able to step back far enough to look at it with some perspective. Jill was able to guide me there.

I opened up about the fears that had come roaring out of hiding. I told her how fear of abandonment and fear of betrayal were by far the most overwhelming and frightening. My fears about being alone and lonely followed close behind. I described how I'd meticulously constructed a world that revolves around my wife and kids, and how nothing else in my life mattered. I talked about how I had no real interests outside of that structure. I said I was devastated, confused and completely lost. I had lived my life in a protective bubble, erecting protective walls so thick that for 46 years I had successfully kept pain and despair at bay. But in the process, I'd also kept anyone from penetrating that barrier—apparently including my wife.

I told Jill everything—except one thing. I couldn't bring myself to tell her about Kelly's indiscretion, even when Jill asked if there was another man in the picture. I don't know what made me hold that back. My ego? The shame of it? The utter humiliation I felt? An impulse to protect Kelly from harsh judgment? Probably all of the above. All I know is that I steered clear of the affair, while candidly describing everything else.

"She keeps saying to me, 'Jonathan, I don't know who you are. For 19 years, whenever I tried to find out, you would get angry, blaming and judging me.' I *do* want to blame her for all of this, but deep down I know I can't. Even knowing that, I can't stop being incredibly angry. She's right, I take everything so personally and don't let anybody in."

Jill was a good listener. She also talked from experience, having twice wrestled with depression. The first brief bout, in her 20's, had prompted her to enter therapy "to get to know [herself] better." In her mid-30s, she'd faced a more protracted bout, triggered by infertility. When her husband refused to consider adoption, she descended into a shattering depression that lasted almost eight months. The happy ending is that she and Joe ultimately adopted a baby girl from China. My beautiful niece, Becky, is now 14. To my eyes, the three of them are living happily ever after. Jill subsequently wrote a wonderful book called *An Empty Lap*. The book charts her road through the infertility nightmare, her intense emotional pain, the strife that nearly ended her marriage, and, ultimately the adoption of Becky. I know I'm biased, but it's a great read. (If you're one of those people suffering through infertility and think you're alone in your torment, this book is an absolute must.)

Anyway, as we walked, Jill listened and probed. Since talking helps me arrange and get a handle on my thoughts, I dumped all that I was thinking about and learning in therapy on her. I was trying to move what I now knew in my brain closer to my heart. For me, that step of moving from the head to the heart is when I know I've put an idea into practice.

Jill gave me the first shred of hope that the pain could go away. "You're light years ahead of where I was," she said. "What you've learned in three or four months took me three or four years to understand in therapy. You're *way* ahead of the game."

I was surprised. All I'd told her was that I had identified the fears that I'd so efficiently buried all my life. Yes, I could articulate them and give them a name. But the flames of hell were still raging, and my panic seemed to be growing.

"I don't get it," I said. "All I feel is pain. Okay, so I've identified the demons. But I don't feel any better. In fact, I feel worse as each day passes. I don't want to wake up anymore. I'm in a death spiral. How can you say I'm 'ahead of the game'? If this is a game, I feel like it's the first inning and I'm losing 15-0, with no outs. The nightmare is that the game will never end and the Devil will keep coming to the plate."

Jill teased me about my lousy sports analogy and we laughed. My serious sister also knows how to lighten an otherwise oppressive atmosphere. It was the first real smile I'd had since Halloween. "I'm serious," she resumed. "It took me years to identify my real issues. You've done it in a mere few months. Don't be so hard on yourself. You're moving through the process at a very rapid pace."

"It feels like forever and it feels like it will never end," I countered. "I don't know how long I can stand this pain."

She jumped all over that. "Do you really think a trauma of this magnitude just comes and goes? You're way down the path to understanding yourself. More important, you are wide open to learning and changing, which most people aren't willing to do. I repeat, don't be so hard on yourself."

She stopped walking, wrapped her arms around me and gave me the most gentle, compassionate hug. She looked at me tenderly and said, "I know how painful this is. Just know that I love you and I'm here for you."

I did what any unsuspecting brother-in-crisis would do: I broke down and cried, with deep racking sobs. I wept for that lonely, traumatized inner child so recently discovered. I wept for the adult who couldn't deal with the depth of his pain and fear. I wept for the husband who missed his wife and best friend so deeply. I wept for the father who couldn't stay strong for his beautiful kids. I wept for the love of my sister. Her compassion and caring gave me the space to fall apart. And I did.

It took me quite a while to pull myself together. Then arm in arm, my big sister and I caught up with the other hikers. No one sensed the emotion of what had just transpired, and Jill would never tell. But for the next six months until the worst of the depression passed, she would call me *every* day—not to preach or lecture or play dime store therapist—but just to check in, just to say, "Hi." If I wanted to talk, her door was always open. If I didn't want to discuss my ongoing battle, she never forced it. She was just there. She'll never know the lifeline she threw me during those horrible months. Her daily phone calls were a salvation. I lived for them. They gave me respite from the horrors of my uncontrolled panic. Those moments gave me sanity. And I became secure in the knowledge that they would come every day.

Looking back, I realize that Jill showed me a whole new concept of love. Her love was not just compassionate; it was selfless and unconditional. I'd always adored my sister. But during those months, my love and respect for her grew a thousand fold.

After that evening's festivities, Kelly and I headed off to the barn. We had given our master suite to my parents. Logistically, it made sense for the two of us to stay in the detached garage apartment.

Sleeping in the barn had potential. As we ascended its staircase, I felt anticipation. She *had* to sleep in the same bed with me as there was no alternative unless she opted for the uncarpeted wood floor. An image of me holding her as we fell asleep filled my head. Idiot that I was, I let my mind take the next illogical step: If we curled up together and spooned, the love would come pouring forth. The fires of hell would be extinguished. The angels would sing. All would be good again.

Wrong.

Though sleep in the same bed we did, that wasn't how the night was meant to go. Fortunately, I was aware enough to sense that cuddling was out of the question. Instead, we talked quietly for a bit, the conversation calm and gentle, our emotional battle lines erased. When the conversation quieted, every nerve ending in my body came alive. "Roll over, idiot, and wrap yourself around her. Hold her close," my mind begged. But Kelly yawned, exclaimed how tired she was, then rolled the other way and went to sleep.

I lay there looking at her back, highlighted by the glow of a full moon. My heart kept skipping beats. She was so beautiful. I found myself once again appreciating her body, which even after three children was still lithe and slim. During the 21 years I'd known her, that beauty had only grown on me. Lying so close, yet not able to touch her, was excruciating.

I watched her sleep a restless sleep. Sometime in the night she started to toss and turn; ultimately she ended up on her stomach. I couldn't stop myself. I reached out and slowly, gently, started to rub her back. It felt to me that the tenderness and love combined with the gentleness and slow movement, relaxed her. She seemed to fall deeper into her dreams. When my arm got tired, I stopped. She was still on her stomach, head facing toward me. Her near hand was resting palm down just below her chin. I covered her hand with mine. This may sound inane, but I was content. I was looking at her, feeling such deep pangs of love. I didn't move for what seemed like hours. Sometime before sunrise, I drifted off.

Kelly awoke with a start. The abruptness of her movement woke me. She looked so tired and vulnerable.

"Hi," I whispered. The sky was light but it was still quite early and the sun wasn't up.

"Hi," she replied. Her tone was heartbreaking, her inflection dropping in the space of that one short syllable. There was no joy in her expression, only sadness.

"Are you all right?" I asked quietly.

"No," she replied, her tone dropping further. "I didn't sleep very well."

"You seemed to settle in to a deep sleep. Not the case?"

"No. You were rubbing my back." She said this without emotion. Her head was down and she was absently staring at a point on the floor somewhere in front of her.

"I thought it would help settle you down. You had been restless. I was worried about you. And you seemed to settle back into a deep sleep while I was rubbing your back." Where was this heading?

Warning sirens screeched in the back of my head. How could I tell her all I wanted to do was sleep with her, touch her, love her, without triggering a caustic response?

The furnace kicked on from the closet downstairs. Intermittent clangs emanated from the pipes. The room was otherwise silent.

"I didn't know how to ask you to stop," she finally said. "I never know how. I panic about saying the wrong thing to you, making you irritated at me. I'm afraid of saying anything because you so often get defensive or misinterpret it. I'm scared of your reactions."

"I'm sorry," I said quietly. "I didn't know. I thought a slow gentle back rub would settle you down. It seemed to be working. It felt good to me."

"It felt good to *you*," she hissed through gritted teeth. "That's the problem. It's *always* about you. What about *me*? Can't you ever think about me?"

Her blistering cannon shot landed smack between my eyeballs. The room started to spin. I tried to speak, but only little gasps came out. It was getting worse, not better. What had happened to the woman I love? Where had she gone? How could things have gotten so bad so fast? I curled into a fetal position and closed my eyes tight against the spinning room. Any thought of further dialogue or intimacy was gone. The tears flowed steadily onto my pillow. I felt pretty damn sorry for myself. How could Kelly be so insensitive? So cruel? All I'd ever done was love her. This was what I got in return? I felt like a lost child.

Even now, the thought of a child having to learn to console himself all alone fills me with pain. At that point in time, I didn't love myself enough to soothe or be gentle with myself. All I could do was wallow in baffled self-pity.

In a child's pain, thoughts hungrily turned to parental support and love. My parents' intimate involvement in my situation was greatly appreciated, but greater exigencies soon dictated that they focus their energies elsewhere. Not long after the 50th anniversary celebration and Thanksgiving festivities, my father suffered a massive heart attack while playing tennis at home back in North Carolina. A quintuple bypass and surgical clean out of both carotid arteries quickly followed. His recovery required undivided attention on both their parts. Then, as my father's health improved, my mother's collapsed. Degenerative arthritis left her in great pain and wheelchair-bound most days. Two vibrant people were facing challenges I'm sure they never bargained for. I needed them desperately, just as they may have needed me. But in the end the best we could do for each other was not lend to each other's' travails; we each had to take care of business separately. Sometimes timing just sucks.

* * *

During the weeks that followed Thanksgiving, the pain attacked frequently and without warning. How could a human being feel this desperate, this anguished, this unhinged? I had not known that a person could experience such devastation, and I had no defense for it. Often, I found myself sobbing on the bathroom floor or in my walk-in closet. No matter where I came apart and no matter how hard I tried, I couldn't hide it from my kids. No child is meant to hear or see his or her father so out of control. Mine did.

It was in this depleted state that I approached the Christmas holidays, which we traditionally spend with my in-laws. Walter and Lea divide their time between Vermont and Florida. Their Vermont house sits on a beautiful mountain property with a spectacular 100-mile view. Christmas in Vermont is always a treat. The house is rustic and simple, built around a brick fireplace. In years past when not skiing, we've always gravitated to that hearth to enjoy the fire's warmth, each other's company and the relaxed, stress-free environment.

Not this year. My oldest son Mike, by now almost 17, didn't join us, opting instead for a snowboard trip out West with his best friend. I was glad we could send him off. At least he got to miss the fireworks. My two youngest, Alex and Sarah, weren't so lucky. Alex and I drove north together, one day behind Kelly and Sarah. As usual, we took two cars to handle all the presents and pets, as well as the kids' busy schedules. That proved to be about the only normal thing about the year's gathering.

My mother-in-law Lea knew that Kelly and I were having trouble. On top of dealing with us, she was taking care of her husband, who was a ways down the path with Alzheimer's. This odious disease had taken my vibrant, successful father-in-law and reduced him to a state of total dependency. Lea was just short of 80 years old. Fully extended, she stood an impressive 4'10". Vivacious and young at heart, she took care of Walter without complaint, while cooking and fussing over all of us. Her love of family, me included, was absolute. Unfortunately, this was the year I destroyed her perfect record of wonderful Christmases.

Alex and I had taken the six hour drive at a leisurely pace and arrived at the Vermont house well after dinner on Christmas Eve. Sarah was there to welcome us with hugs and kisses and her beautiful smile. Kelly's older sister and her two girls hadn't made the trip up from their home in Florida, but her younger sister, Susan, a die-hard Vermonter, was also there to greet us. Lea and Kelly followed. Walt was sleeping, something he was now doing almost 20 hours a day.

Alex and I unpacked the car and deposited everything in the front hall. As the house is relatively small, the whole Lewis clan had a tradition of bunking together in the upstairs bedroom. The kids would sleep on the floor, thick with blankets and quilts, while Kelly and I would commandeer the two single beds, which we would push together for the week.

With bags in hand, I started up the stairs, headed for the bedroom. Kelly followed me up and said, "I've set up a bed for you on the floor in the study. I think it's best you stay in there." Though her tone was neutral, everything started to spin. It hadn't occurred to me that we would sleep apart in her parents' house. My mind raced in terror. We had slept together in the barn over Thanksgiving when my family had gathered, hadn't we? It was, if nothing else, a show of solidarity and harmony in the face of family. Why was this any different? Kelly was talking but I couldn't hear what she was saying. I was hyperventilating. All that registered was the terror that had seized me like a chokehold. In that moment, the world as I knew it ended. In that moment, I lost all hope. What was worse, in the coming months, I would learn that the moment didn't have an ending.

Seeing my fear and confusion, perhaps even scared for me, Kelly took me by the arm and, still talking, talking, led me to the study. There it was—my prison cell. I resisted stepping through the door. I was being locked up, punished. This wasn't right. I was innocent. There must be a mistake. I hadn't done anything wrong. Why was she torturing me like this?

My eyes must have been dilated with fear. I know I continued to hyperventilate. Everything remained out of focus. Kelly hovered over me and seemed concerned. She was fussing over me, trying to settle me down. It didn't make any sense.

Then I was alone. It was just me, locked away in a jail worse than any hell I'd ever imagined. I couldn't catch my breath, couldn't lay still, couldn't think clearly. I was beyond panicked. Everything had come unglued.

The only other thing I remember about the rest of that night was Kelly coming into the room more than once. She was angry that I was crying and that her mother could hear me downstairs. She wanted me to pull myself together "for the sake of her family." I had no reserve either to answer her or to stop the tears.

What does Christmas morning evoke for you? Though I'm Jewish, and Kelly and I are raising our kids as such, Christmas for us was always a joyous time. My in-laws made it so special. Lots of presents, laughter and the excitement of the kids energizing the space. It was all about family and love and sharing. I loved being married and being able to celebrate this wonderful holiday.

This Christmas was anything but joyous. I don't think I ever fell asleep the night before, lying there in the study all by myself. Christmas morning only prolonged the nightmare. I sat in the rocker lounger next to the fire while we all opened presents. Alex and Sarah were the only two excited people in the house but that didn't dampen their enthusiasm. Given different circumstances, I would have been just as excited.

Given *these* circumstances, it was all I could do to sit upright. I was in such a daze that I couldn't even fake a smile for the kids' sake. Lea looked so sad. Here it was Christmas morning, and there was her daughter looking completely lost, and her son-in-law falling apart before her eyes. No mother should have to see her loved ones going through such agony.

Alex gave me the nicest Christmas present of all. Several times that morning, and again throughout the week, he found quiet time to come up and wrap his beautiful arms around me. No words were necessary. The hugs were from his soul. His tenderness touched me deeply. I only wish he didn't have to see me so broken.

Christmas night was a repeat of the one before. I couldn't sleep. Hell, I couldn't breathe, think or function either. All I could do was curl up in a tight fetal position and try not to cry too loudly. God forbid anyone should hear me, thus prompting Kelly to scold me for not being stronger. In the end, I was again unsuccessful.

December 26th is a day I will never forget, much as I'd like to. I arose with my panic at a feverish pitch. I was incapable of speaking or eating. I couldn't face my kids or my in-laws. The pain was so raw that sitting still was impossible. By mid-morning, I couldn't stand it any longer. I pulled on my boots, hat and ski jacket, and, forgetting my gloves, headed out onto the mountain. I took Sam, Lea's frisky golden retriever, with me.

With my hands tucked deep in my jeans pockets, Sam and I headed up the hill. Dogs are wonderful companions. They love you no matter what. Sam was so happy to be out in the snow with me. He didn't understand that I was in no shape to romp or stomp with him. So he did what any good dog would do: he rolled around in the snow by himself for a while, then playfully jumped up on me. Sam weighs over 90 pounds. Match his enthusiasm with his size, add the fact that my hands were buried in my pockets, and the result was a tangle of human limbs and dog parts as the whole mess hit the snow.

Thanks, I needed that.

I lay in the snow, gripped by another wave of panic. My hands were still in my pockets, with snow trickling down my back. I felt nothing. Sam was standing over me licking my face, tail wagging. He just wanted to play. I just wanted to lie there. What a mismatch we were. I think I even laughed at the absurdity of the moment. I tugged my hands from my Levis and dragged Sam down into the snow to play.

My hands were numb when Sam and I got back to the house, but for a short while I think I was actually conscious. I ate lunch, much to Lea's pleasure. She'd never seen me decline food before, as I had on Christmas day. I played a game of Risk with Alex, Sarah and Kelly. I even settled down to read a book I'd received on Christmas. For a few short hours, there was a semblance of normalcy.

It didn't last long. By mid-afternoon the anxiety returned with a vengeance. In part it was the close proximity of the woman I loved who remained at such a removed place. In part it was the vice-like grip of my own unfettered insecurities. Who knows what else played into it. All I know is that my terror bubbled up with little warning, bigger and angrier than anything I had felt up to this point. Kelly saw my frantic distress and said something, I have no idea what. I could manage only, "I gotta get out of here," before I bolted for the door.

I hit the driveway running. Whatever had taken hold of me was ugly, really ugly, and it wasn't letting go. I was a couple of hundred yards up the dirt road, out of sight of the house, when it erupted. By the time Kelly reached me, I was on all fours howling hysterically, like a rabid animal. This wasn't a crying jag. It was insanity.

I screamed. Without control. For a very long time.

I was in another dimension. The only sane thought to penetrate my terror was, "This must be what happens when someone snaps. This must be what going mad looks like. This must be the moment when men in white coats come to take you away."

I kept screaming, blood-curdling screams. Poor Kelly. Although she was my torturer and the catalyst of this horror show, this had never been her intent. She never really wanted to hurt me, something I wouldn't understand until many months later. It was just her own stuff she had to deal with, but didn't know how. Right now, though, she had to deal with this crazy man who was taking the brunt of her flailing efforts. She was probably afraid to leave me alone in that state; certainly she was incapable of doing anything to bring me down. She just rubbed my back, or at least that's what she was doing when some semblance of sanity returned.

Had an hour gone by? Two? My throat hurt and my stomach ached. I was sweating profusely despite the single-digit temperature. I wound down slowly, like a spinning top losing momentum. As all systems slowed, my brain started to sputter back into gear. Kelly's hand was on my back, I recognized that. I was on the ground on all fours. That was weird. I felt very light-headed.

Reality crashed into my consciousness with such force that it literally knocked me off all fours. I keeled over into the snow, curling into a tight ball. And I wept. Not the way I had been crying all these months, but from a place much deeper within. I could taste the grief. My terror had given way to heartache.

When the tears subsided, I couldn't speak. I just looked up at Kelly the way an injured dog looks beseechingly to his master for help. "Take care of me," was the message. She understood.

Quietly she asked if I was ready to go back to the house. It was gentle and kind – empathy I wouldn't see directed at me again for months and months to come. When I nodded, she helped me up and we started the short, silent walk back. In the front hall I peeled off my outer clothing, then made my way up the stairs to the study—my prison cell. I couldn't face the kids, much less my in-laws, so I hid in that horrible room with all its heartbreaking implications.

I was numb when Kelly came into the room. For the first time since her breakaway in August, she seemed caring and compassionate. She spoke softly and with tenderness. Her gentle concern registered through the haze. I took no hope from it, but it felt wonderful nonetheless.

"Are you going to be okay?" she asked. I nodded, my eyes closing with the effort. "What can I do to help?" I shook my head from side to side, inhaling and exhaling with shallow, labored breaths. With deep sadness in her eyes she whispered, "I'm so sorry." Then she left.

Deflated and exhausted, I lay there, staring at nothing. I was too wound up to sleep, too broken to think. If any thought registered, it was simply, "I can't go on." The catatonia lasted through the night. I don't remember moving a muscle. I don't remember sleeping either. When the sun came up, I rallied enough to go down for breakfast, where I sat with a cup of coffee and stared blankly into the fire. Kelly, the kids, my mother-in-law all tried without success to draw me into conversation. Sarah and Alex must have been so confused.

By lunch, Alex and Sarah convinced me to play another game of Risk. I lasted a few rounds more this time, but my armies couldn't rally and ultimately got crushed. I guess I was never meant to take over the world. That was Alex's calling. Sarah was feisty and battled on, but big brother ruled. It was heartening to see them having such a good time, and to know that my mood wasn't dampening their warrior spirits.

I was back in the rocker by the fireplace when it hit again. Kelly's detachment had already broken my heart. Now, it broke my spirit. Like the day before, it was all I could do to get out the door and far enough up the hill to not scare the kids before I began screaming. At some point in the breakdown, Kelly again came to my side and again rubbed my back. At what point I even registered that she was there remains a mystery. But when I did, what I saw in her face was her own terror. I had broken apart completely, unable to handle what she claimed was a communication problem in our marriage. Despite her ongoing words about what she didn't feel for me and what she did feel for the electrician, she did often exhort in obnoxiously cavalier tones that we would eventually talk through and resolve the problem. Her strong, confident husband could never fall apart, or certainly not this completely.

"I need help," I whispered. "I need medical help. Maybe I should get myself admitted to a hospital. I'm coming apart. I can't handle this."

This is where all memory stops. I know what transpired over the next few hours only because it was described to me later. Kelly got me back to the house and immediately called Janet. Janet has an M.S. in counseling, and therefore lacks the medical qualifications to prescribe drugs. So she connected Kelly with a psychiatrist she trusted who specializes in psychopharmacology. Apparently, he spoke at length with me by phone. Normal times would have required an office visit first. But this was an emergency. Since I was in Vermont and he was down in Pennsylvania, he phoned in a prescription for a quick-fix cocktail of sleeping pills and anti-anxiety medication to the local pharmacy. The office visit would have to wait until I returned.

It turns out that anti-anxiety medication takes at least two weeks before its effects kick in. Since I wasn't around for observation, maybe the doctor was hoping that a placebo effect would take hold. You know: if the patient *thinks* he's getting a miracle remedy, the result is just as potent. On the other hand, he may have told me about the medication's delayed efficacy. I don't remember. All I know is that the sleeping pills worked, knocking me out and giving me my first rest in months. By morning, I was back from the land of lunacy. The terror of losing my wife and its associated trauma, however, was still there in all its living color.

I would have many more outbursts over the next 15 months. As in Vermont, when the fits of screaming would descend, they would hit with a vengeance that was beyond my ability to control. None of those episodes, though, would put me over the edge the way the Christmas breakdown did. As Kelly and I headed back to Doylestown in separate cars, separate universes, I understood that I was at risk of losing my wife, my life, my very sanity. I needed to deal with my problems. But I still wasn't ready.

5. WINTER OF DESPAIR

When we returned from Vermont, Kelly told me that she wanted separation. Not *a* separation. Separation, as in physical space. Translation: She'd decided to sleep in the barn. The torture I'd experienced at her parents' place was apparently only just beginning. She was so cold, so walled in her concrete bunker. Since she wouldn't talk to me, I began a one-way conversation with God, mixing my silent appeals of, "Why does this have to be so painful?" with, "Please don't let her leave me. I'll be in your service forever if you just make us all right again." This is what's known in the grief trade as "bargaining." At the time it felt like pure desperation.

I longed for Kelly—but she was a million emotional miles away and still retreating. I was a wreck. No wife. No longer a job worth speaking of. No self-esteem. No sense of self-worth. Not only couldn't I find my core, I wondered if I'd ever had one. Kelly's pain and sadness were also becoming clearer to me. Every fiber in me wanted to comfort and hold her. But she kept saying in a smug, disgusted tone, "All that does is make *you* feel better." I blindly assumed she must be right. That left me questioning whether my love for her was toxic, as she kept insisting.

Too uncomfortable to sit still, I began pouring my misery into a journal. "I can't think, I can barely function. I'm moving through the days like a robot and barely able to work. Is the life I thought I loved dead? Do I say *Kaddish* [the Jewish prayer for the dead] for myself? I feel ashamed."

I frantically wanted Kelly back, not in the way that it used to be, but in a new and vibrant relationship. But my anger—my shield against facing the crushing prospect that she might actually leave me—kept getting in the way of reasonable discussion. I should specify that my lashings were verbal, not physical. It feels absurd to say that, since it would never occur to me to lay an angry hand on Kelly or anyone else for that matter. But I want no misunderstanding, since by now Kelly was talking frequently of how she "feared" my anger, language she had perhaps learned while counseling battered women.

When I was with Kelly, I was bitter, judgmental, harsh and accusing. My anger came out in biting words – callous, sarcastic in-your-face blame. When I was alone, I blamed myself. In my journal, I wrote:

> The shame is so deep. Kelly, how do I truly let you know how sorry I am? Words are useless. I can only show you by my actions, by growing up and taking responsibility for myself – completely. I don't know how to do that. All I know is my uncontrollable anger at this injustice. Please, please, please find the forgiveness in your heart – a forgiveness that I am unsuccessfully trying to find in my own. It's more than I have a right to ask. I now understand how deeply I've hurt you across the years, but I just never knew. I am so in love with you – and I just didn't know any better. Please give me the time to show you – and myself. I love you. Now I have to learn to love me.

Since I was still getting little sleep, I saw the psycho-pharmacologist as soon as I returned from Vermont. He said I was suffering from deep anxiety, not depression. Terrific. He also changed my sleeping medication. But like the original prescription, it worked for only a few hours a night, when it worked at all. I was constantly tired, still dropping weight, still moving through each day like a zombie. I wanted so badly to turn in a more positive direction. But I couldn't find the bottom from which to push off. On New Year's Eve, summoning every bit of inspiration and psychobabble I'd gleaned from assorted self-help and philosophy books, I wrote:

> Be gentle with myself. Love me for who and what I am. Let the collapse just happen and deal with it compassionately and tenderly. The universe will take care of me. Just accept that, live only in the moment ... My job isn't in jeopardy.... Kelly isn't leaving me. All will work out. Just focus on the new me. Love each moment only. Happy New Year to me.

I didn't believe a word of it.

I found myself staring often at her photo on my nightstand. Each time I would be swept by such huge waves of emotion. She looked too beautiful in the picture. I finally threw it into a drawer. I just wanted to forget. I just wanted her.

It is said that there is no such thing as coincidence. Take my job, for instance. If I hadn't been reduced to a territory salesman, I never could have survived at work. By working from a home-based office, no one knew what I did with my days—or didn't. Results were all that mattered. But as the economy had taken a bad turn, the tech business was slow everywhere. The brass, those I once called peers, all knew it would take a year or two to turn on the new niche I was selling into. As a result, I was able to hide for the better part of a year, and no one suspected a thing.

On New Year's Day, a timely opportunity dropped in my lap during a phone conversation with my old business friend, Dan. Once a raging alcoholic, Dan had hit rock bottom 11 years earlier. "Only at the bottom can you be honest about yourself," he often said. "I had to admit to myself that I was powerless over alcohol, that my life had become unmanageable, before I was ready to help myself." Only much later would I learn that he was quoting the first step of AA's *Twelve Step Recovery* program. He got a sponsor and became active in AA; took a leave of absence from his job and hiked all 2,162 miles of the Appalachian Trail; trained for and ran in marathons, never having run a step prior to going sober. Along the way, he and his wife divorced. Dan, who has since remarried, is now a happy man, diligent about living a simple, balanced and healthy life, passionate about "giving back" by helping others. He is a wonderful example of a man in crisis who, through grit and determination, turned his life around. He is my role model.

So I listened attentively as Dan told me about a series of workshops run by therapists of varying specialties for adults suffering from painful situations usually tied to some sort of addiction. He and several of his AA buddies had been through the main workshop, with excellent results. The purpose of these classes was to help small groups of people get to the root of their dysfunctions and fears. After we hung up, I followed Dan's advice and took a look at the web site. When I called the next morning to see if I could get in to a future workshop, I was told that my timing was perfect: there was one remaining slot for a five-day intensive workshop that was beginning three days hence. Must be fate.

Later that day, I took a phone interview. Since the program's therapists believe in the adage, "You can only help those who help themselves," the interview was required to confirm that the prospective attendee had the right frame of mind and refused to give up until he achieved the quality of life that he thought he deserved. As best I could, I explained my trauma and what had triggered it. I described the depth of my despair, and my inability to pull myself out of it. When the voice asked, "Have you ever considered suicide?" I lamely joked, "What depressed, deeply anxiety-ridden person wouldn't?" I continued, "In my life I had *never* considered it. Now I consider throwing myself in front of every car that comes at me while I'm out running. But I'd never do it. I have three beautiful kids. I'd never do that to them. I have too much respect for them to be that drastic. Besides, somewhere in my fog I know I have too much to live for. I just don't see it right now."

"You're our kind of guy," the voice trilled. "Come on down!"

The Maryland countryside provided a peaceful setting, free of external influences or interruptions. A rustic old farm house served as classroom, dining facility and domicile; we weren't permitted to leave the premises without an escort.

The workshop was small and intimate, just eight participants. Five were addicted to alcohol, two to food, one—me—to his wife. We gave our collective misery a rigorous workout. The classes dealt with addiction, dysfunction, neglect and abuse, and the wounds we consciously or unconsciously bare. We discussed and play-acted situations that interfered with our ability to lead healthy, productive lives. We addressed distorted self-image, low self-esteem, enabling and controlling behavior, irrational beliefs and unhealthy relationship patterns. We tackled anger, depression, resentment, guilt, shame, sadness, abandonment, and, oh yes, loss of spontaneity and joy.

Within the group setting, attention was given to each person's issues. We were told to let go and see where it would take us. The goal was to drive each of us to our center, our own unique core, in order to develop "what needs developing." After you face your real issues, the therapists told us, you then need to shift your "dance." For me, that meant changing *my* half of the dance, while understanding that I couldn't change Kelly's. It was a hard concept to swallow; I'd never taken to the dance floor on my own.

Journal – Tuesday, January 7 - morning before class

I feel a little lost and still a lot sad. Sleep escapes me here too. I'm tired and don't feel at all grounded. It would be so nice to find my footing, find myself. I'm just hoping that this week will help me start to respect myself and feel good about who I am. Right now, I don't.

The group discussions have been nice. It's helpful to know that I'm not crazy. Others have told me that they really respect the tenacity and openness with which I'm approaching this workshop. Me? I just want to find joy within myself. I can't go on suffering like this.

I love Kelly so much. She's always in my thoughts. I need to separate from that much more this week – stay focused on me. Even in group, I'm still lonely. What's that all about?

The psychologists and therapists tossed around lots of buzz words to give definition to my "addiction." But I hated being labeled. My comrades-in-misery, who had spent years owning up to their problems, heaped praise on me for even being at the workshop, just five months into my "addiction." That gave me no solace.

Still, I cried unabashedly all week and expended tremendous energy trying to understand enough so I could *begin* to get a grip on myself. Though the various messages didn't reach my heart, a lot did come clear in my head. During those intensive days, I finally began to understand what I'd heard so often, without effect, in therapy: I needed to stand on my own two feet. I needed to find out who I was and become comfortable with that person. I needed to learn to enjoy life for me, not for or because of anybody else. I needed to develop interests of my own. In short, I needed to become responsible for my own happiness.

The bad news was that all of this ratcheted up my panic. I'd never before been accountable for my own time. I'd never lived alone. Never had an open-ended schedule. Never developed any hobbies. Never taken responsibility for my own time. Never even stopped to consider if I *had* any personal needs unconnected to my loved ones. Throughout my life, I'd leaned first on the family I grew up in, and then on the family I'd helped to create, to provide me with a sense of fulfillment. My unarticulated motto was, "Just tell me what to do and I'll be happy." And all along the way, I'd thought I was. Now, my deepest terror was staring right at me: my fear of being alone. How the hell was I supposed to start wrestling this monster to the mat?

The good news was that I could now articulate my darkest fear. *That,* I suppose, *was* the start. And it was petrifying. Before leaving the workshop, I wrote in my journal:

> I can't breathe. I'm afraid of going home. What will I face? I miss Kelly so much that it hurts to my very core. But I now understand that I have to focus on me and put my relationship with her to the side. I just don't want to do that. I want her love, her friendship and her passion. I can't accept the constant "We just miss" comments. All she can give me right now is friendship – and there are no signs that she will find her way back to a loving or caring or passionate marriage. I cannot accept symbiotic friendship when there is nothing pointing to reconciliation. It's cruel and inhuman to say that friendship is all you are willing and able to do. Where is the compromise?… All I ever wanted was to be loved. I thought I had that. I know now that I don't. But I have to trust the process. If I say it enough times, maybe I'll actually be able to find the faith to accept the situation and let it run its natural course.

Nothing had changed—but everything had changed. I wasn't at all comfortable with the circumstances to which I returned at home. But for the first time, I was catching fleeting glimpses of what gains and changes might accrue from my trauma. Despite the pain, I sensed the growth and freedom that would ultimately result. Somehow, the combination of the workshop, the marital therapy, my reading and my confrontation with my fears were affording me ephemeral moments of understanding. It wasn't acceptance by any stretch—but it was a start.

For the first time, I looked at my situation as a loss, a death that needed to be grieved. Kelly had said that more than a few times over the months. But, as with most things pertaining to our relationship, I was incapable of hearing it from her.

In the weeks that followed the workshop, I ping-ponged between shock, abandonment fears, depression, rage and massive doses of denial—all well-documented stages of grief. But even in my more lucid moments, I was still light years away from the final stage: acceptance. Acceptance takes some self-esteem, I think. And that was a characteristic that continued to elude me entirely. So, despite the brief glimpses of light, the panic attacks continued.

Journal Entry

I want so badly to be loved and cherished and felt passionate about. And it's certainly not coming from Kelly. We talked deeply and openly throughout the weekend. That part was at least refreshing – to know that I could control the rage I feel about her disconnection for at least one conversation. But she is vocal and firm: she is *not* in love with me nor does she feel at all passionate about me. However, if I were strong, she said, if I were an 'alpha male', she could see herself coming around. She wants me completely in charge of my own life. She doesn't want any part of a caretaker/nurturer role. By being separate and standing strong and alone, only then can we come back together. Gag me with a fucking spoon. In one breath she says she's scared of me because I'm too strong and in the next that she wants me to be her alpha male. I don't get it.

...She says my love for her is needy, not clean. She says she doesn't want the responsibility. She wants strength, someone she can lean on, someone to challenge her emotionally, spiritually and intellectually. And right now, that ain't me.

I need to get a grip on myself. I must find the strength to live on my own terms and not be so dependent on her – which I know I am. It's killing me...She says she's not leaving – why doesn't that make it any easier? It's actually harder with her around but separate as a constant reminder of my passion for her at every turn. I am struggling so hard. Kelly replies, "This shouldn't be a struggle at all ... it's perfect, just the way it's supposed to be ..."

This shouldn't be a struggle? Our bust-up was perfect? At this point, I was so far gone that I didn't even hear how absurd she sounded. Instead, I wrote, "Easy for her to say. Insensitive too. I am screaming for help. Is anybody listening?"

One friend was. She suggested that I get a "reading" done by a woman named Sheila whom she knew and trusted. Why not, I thought. When all else fails, try something different. For me, this wasn't even all that much of a stretch. I firmly believe in the sixth sense, psychic phenomenon, the paranormal, ESP. I just don't trust all the freak shows out there. So while I approached my appointment with Sheila with a healthy amount of skepticism, I was open to the possibilities. I wasn't disappointed.

Sheila's office was small and simple, filled with books, two cushy lounge chairs, an old desk and several plants. A desk lamp was on but the overhead fluorescents were not, giving the room a warm glow. There were no crystals, no incense pots, no other weird shit. Sheila herself looked the motherly sort, dressed in a practical pants suit, her hair short and cut simply. She wore no perceptible makeup and no crazy baubles, amulets or jewelry. She spoke quietly and without any hint of arrogance or creepy "all-knowing." She inspired trust.

As we settled into facing lounge chairs, she explained her process to me. She was a channel for another worldly entity, a guide so to speak. He would talk (channel) through her given the right circumstance. This meant there was no guarantee he would come through, but she was comfortable with that possibility and hoped I understood. She told me she would tape the session so I wouldn't have to take notes. With that, she turned the cassette player on, took a deep cleansing breath, then closed her eyes and went silent.

The first few sentences from her guide put any lingering doubts to rest. "You are presently transforming at all levels of your being. Set your mind to completing this transition... Think about transforming your emotions, especially anger, into creativity... There is a creative solution; you just don't know it... Don't be paralyzed with regret."

Well, that hit the nail on the head.

The guide's next points revolved around my fear. "You can *no longer* figure out with your mind what to do next. You fear losing control, a fear of surrendering and letting go. You believe that if you surrender now, you'll lose the whole 'war.' But it is essential and you must do it without self-blame...It's about letting go of being able to fix it." I took this to mean my marriage.

He said that I hadn't been happy for a long time but accepted it, then buried it and made it all right. "You will find relief to stop pretending. Stop pretending to be happy. Focus on what is important and what you truly want for yourself and your family... It is not of benefit to continue to suffer." He was clear that I needed to trust my deeper feelings about what I needed to do. He was clear that I needed to stop turning away and hoping that the problem would go away... Release the energy to deal with each day *as it comes*. He said that there was potential loss but tremendous gain of something I didn't know yet.

He spent a lot of time on the point that *not* knowing what will happen develops faith and trust. Through not knowing, I would find the creative solution. It was back to the concept of "being present" and "in the moment"—but he had the good grace not to use those annoying phrases. "Free yourself; feel the loss of control; feel that you can no longer hold on to it all. *Surrender*. It's okay not to know." Then he offered an analogy that finally made the point real for me:

> *"Consider your circumstance as if you've fallen into the rapids of a raging river. You have choice. You can fight the power of the violent water or, you can choose to put your feet in front of you and give in totally to it and let the power of the river take you where it may. With the former, you are certain to get buffeted wildly around, slamming into rocks and other objects along the way. You are bound to get badly hurt in your effort to save yourself. Or you can choose the latter. In that scenario of letting go, the water will take you gracefully between the rocks and debris and deposit you unharmed into the calm waters at the rapids' end. Then, and only then, when everything is calm and in control, would you take over and swim comfortably to safety."*

That made sense to me. I was bucking the tide and suffering the consequences, getting smacked around hard. I couldn't accept the situation and let it play itself out. Instead, I was trying to steer it to the only conclusion I wanted: a rejuvenated, passionate,

intimate marriage. But there are so many paths to that conclusion…and so many other possible conclusions.

At the session's end, he reminded me once more, "It is *not*
about handling it! Let go of handling it. Trust and have faith that
the universe will guide you appropriately."

I could have saved myself a whole lot of pain and suffering if
I had taken the lesson to heart at that time. I guess I just wasn't
ready yet.

Oh boy, more pain.

In February, my son Alex and I joined several members of my
family on a week-long ski trip out West. The day we flew home,
Kelly left for a two-week visit to her parents in Florida. As a result,
I didn't see her for three weeks. The day before she was to return
home, we had a phone conversation that was symptomatic of our
inability to communicate with each other in a way that the other
could hear.

"I'm nervous about coming home," she said, sounding
vulnerable.

My response was heartfelt. "Please don't worry, sweetheart. I
think I've come to grips with giving you the space you've been asking for but I've been unable to give these many months. You won't
feel any pressure. I mean that. Please don't be nervous."

I thought my response was empathetic and reasonable. But she
got really mad, chastising me, saying that I didn't acknowledge her
concern. I went right to a solution …again …without considering
her need. Her attack really caught me up short. She wanted space,
and I was offering it. Why was I being lectured? Why such an ugly
tone? I felt like she was undermining and manipulating me no
matter which way I danced.

Frustrated and confused, I took it to Janet the next day in
therapy. "Jonathan, stop trying to fix everything," she said. "It's

not that you did anything wrong; you just didn't acknowledge her feelings."

Annoyed, I responded, "I feel like I'm damned if I do and damned if I don't. Wasn't I responding with what she had been asking for—an offer of emotional space? This feels just like the rebuke I got when I suggested that she take some aspirin after she said she had a headache. Or the reprimand when she walked through the kitchen and commented that she couldn't find her sneakers. I responded, 'Have you checked the mudroom closet?' which elicited an angry reply that she wasn't asking me for a solution. What am I missing?"

"In another relationship, Jonathan, your answers would have been fine. But you two consistently trigger each other. Kelly has repeatedly said that she feels controlled and overpowered by you, and that you don't hear what it is she is saying. She feels invisible to you. You don't acknowledge who she is or what she says. Rather, you make everything about you."

"I do make a lot of things about me," I allowed. "I'm working on it. She knows that. But the examples I gave don't fit. In those situations, I didn't make anything about me. Suggesting the aspirin or checking out the mudroom closet were just natural, helpful responses. Saying that I would give her the space she's been begging for *was* acknowledging her fear."

"Stop trying *to do*," Janet replied. "Be the receiver. Kelly so desperately needs to be heard, acknowledged for who and what she is. It is far more important for her to know that you really hear her than to tell her what to do. The aspirin and closet examples smack of you telling her what to do. That is her reality. It doesn't make it right or wrong. Experience her pain, not your own for a while."

At that moment, all I could think was Mars…Venus…

There was one positive idea noodling around in my brain at this time: The motorcycle license. Constantly, Russ nudged me to sign up for the Pennsylvania Department of Transportation's free safety course scheduled for that spring. Initially, I felt torn between Russ's enthusiasm and the guilt that comes from a mother's life-long admonitions. But with all the hell raging in my life, I finally sided with the potential for some enjoyment. Thirty days before the class was to start and on the first day of registration, I dialed the DOT phone number at exactly 9:00 a.m. and was the first person to schedule for the early April class.

On a cold, wet Sunday afternoon in March, Kelly called me over to the barn where she had taken up residence. I trudged dutifully across the driveway and up the stairs into the apartment. She looked horrible. In a pitiful tone, she said that she'd been crying all day. "We just miss," she hissed for the thousandth time.

To me, she looked and sounded theatrical. It felt like I was watching a grade B actress deliver a soliloquy from a grade B soap opera. Looking back, I should have known better. Kelly was completely lost and unable to make sense of her situation. She was probably doing the best she could. But I was learning - I kept my big mouth shut.

"I feel dead," she continued. "I'm exhausted. I need a place where I can rest. I can't take it any more."

She had repeated those same phrases 10,000 times since the disconnect. It did nothing to move me closer to her. It sounded so...well, theatrical. Instead of taking in the reality of her pain, I felt manipulated and defensive. Still, I kept my mouth shut.

"I can't go on," she moaned. "It's over."

She didn't use the 'D' word, but the implication was clear. Now, I couldn't have responded even if I'd wanted to. She had rendered me mute. That evening I wrote:

I guess I'm getting divorced. It's said – I guess it's done. It's the last thing I want. I want the love of my wife back. It won't happen now....How can I fight city hall? My love and passion for her is obviously not enough – it's a one-way street.

Divorce – I just can't believe it. It seems so surreal. How can one person love another so much and have nothing come back except pity?

How do I "stay present"? How is this supposed to be "just perfect"? Such bullshit. Another newly minted second-career psychotherapist goes to divorce court. Seems like it's a requirement of the profession. I was certainly warned about it.

Though I'd held my tongue that time, my anger was pushing her further and further away. Every time we talked, I seemed to go off the deep end, which then set her off. The statements that most consistently launched me into tirade mode were those in which she told me how I *should* have responded, ones like: "For 20 years I would try to tell you how I felt about something between us but all you would do is get defensive and angry. You never say, 'Hey that's interesting, Kelly. I hear you saying that my anger pushes you away. Tell me more'." It made me crazy. Still does. What I always *heard* was how she had it all figured out, but that I wasn't coming around, didn't understand, heard only what I wanted to hear, then got angry and critical about it.

Who knows. Maybe that's what *she* heard when I offered my unsolicited advice on matters great and small. Maybe it was just her own insecurities. What I do know is that she couldn't hear past my anger, which was merciless as I blamed, judged and criticized. And I couldn't hear past her condescending all-knowing tone of voice, which pushed my anger button. My hottest button would get pressed when she went off into what she thought of as a heightened state of spirituality, and I thought of as Woo Woo Land. When in Woo Woo Land, Kelly's eyes would look wide to the heavens, and her voice would become breathy. Her hands would either cover her heart or be clasped in prayer in front of her. Starry-eyed, she would whisper, "The universe is changing and we need to change with it. The universe is so much bigger than we are. Our [divorce] problems are so irrelevant in comparison. We need to see the bigger picture." Who the hell is she kidding? *Earth to Kelly...*

But when in Woo Woo Land, there was no pulling Kelly back to the realities of our situation. "Look at what you have instead of what you don't have," she would say, her voice tinged with awe.

"Tell me what I have," I'd respond irritably.

"A marriage in crisis."

If that didn't do the trick (and it never did), she'd shift to another favorite Woo Woo tactic. "I'm not outcome related," she'd intone. "I only care about having the right relationship with you. I don't care whether it's in a marriage or not. The world is in such trouble. It's so much more important that the relationship is right."

What fucking universe did *she* spawn from?

Thus came another wake-up call from the cosmos, timed too perfectly to seem coincidental. I picked up a marvelous book by Gary Zukav called *The Seat of the Soul* that thoughtfully delivers a credible New Age message. He starts from the premise that you believe in the existence of your soul. He talks about "Authentic Power," which he defines as the alignment of your personality with your soul. He believes that Authentic Power is inherent in each of us; we just need to reach out for it.

Zukav makes the case that your soul longs for harmony, cooperation, sharing and reverence for life. That's easy enough to buy into. It's the next part that struck me.

"The parts of your personality that oppose these interactions are the parts that are frightened. They are the parts that are angry, vengeful, jealous, depressed, compulsive, obsessed and addicted."

Hmm, maybe someone had given him my phone number?

"An individual who lives a fulfilling and meaningful life is not tormented by fears and vulnerabilities. He has no need to defend himself or criticize another."

This certainly caught me up short. I had no doubt that I was tormented by fears and vulnerabilities. By now, I even understood that I lived my life protecting and defending myself from them. I used my anger to cover my vulnerability. I was highly critical of so many things, all of which Kelly felt, absorbed and finally snapped over.

"Painful emotions have causes. These causes are internal, not external. Avoiding painful emotions prevents the exploration of their causes."

Again he struck a chord. I was running as hard as I could *not* to face my pain. I just wanted it to go away.

"Fear of any sort is resistance to emotional awareness... Use a situation you don't want to be in as an opportunity to feel what you are feeling.... Each diversion away from a painful emotion halts a process that longs to be completed. Each painful emotion is a doorway leading to a destination you were born to attain. When you mask, obscure or anesthetize an emotion, you turn your back on the doorway."

Bingo. All I had ever done was to squash my fears down, hide them, make like they didn't exist. God forbid someone should find out—especially me. I was turning my back on that described doorway and, as a result, blowing my marriage. So how does one change?

> "To change your life you must accept your life. This appears to be a paradox but it is not. Once you accept your life – greet it without resistance – you can determine what you need to change in order to create the circumstances and experiences you desire.
>
> Changing your life means being present in it, moment by moment. Changing your life begins with accepting your life as it is. When you do that, you are in a position to change."

Light bulbs should have been going off above my head. But no, I got hung up on that irritating phrase about "being present." And I certainly was not ready to accept my life as it was. It sucked. I had always been taught to control tomorrow's outcome; create the image; sculpt my own persona. I just couldn't accept "take it as it comes" quite yet.

So, the cosmos tried again, this time dropping in my lap Greg Bauer's book *Real Love: The Truth about Finding Unconditional Love and Fulfilling Relationships.* Bauer came at me from a different angle.

> "People who don't feel unconditionally loved are desperate and will do almost anything to eliminate the pain of their emptiness ... other people hurt us only because they're reacting badly to the pain of feeling unloved and alone."

Kelly was clear that I had saved her when I married her. She was trying to escape all that she disdained in her life, and I had come to the rescue, her knight in shining armor. Put another way:

she was looking for unconditional love, something she had never experienced. Me, I was reacting badly to her disconnect because I couldn't deal with the pain of feeling unloved and alone. This Bauer guy made perfect sense. But why would anger be my response?

> "Our anger is actually a reaction to the feelings of helplessness and fear that result from a lifetime of struggling to survive without unconditional love...The anger we feel towards our partners results from past events and present decisions... Anger protects us and makes us feel better ... briefly."

I was choosing to be angry. Absolutely. And getting angry *did* make me feel better...briefly. Inevitably, regret followed. I saw this, I understood this, I digested this. But it would still be another year before I was ready to accept my fate and flow with it, the prerequisite to enduring change.

6. SPRING OF CONFUSION

As we headed into spring, things did not improve much. But we kept trying.

One Friday in early May, Kelly went out to breakfast with Stephanie, the wife half of a couple with whom we were good friends. That afternoon, she mentioned to me that she'd "told all" over coffee. Up till now, few people knew about our troubles. How much had she shared about our marital woes? The electrician? Her disconnect?

That night, Kelly and I tried out a new Thai restaurant that had just opened in town to excellent reviews. That she agreed to spend the evening with me was a positive sign. After dropping 30 pounds, I was finally eating again. A dinner out seemed a nice change of pace. After placing our orders, I asked, "So what *did* you tell Stephanie?"

"I told her nothing that I haven't told you already," she replied.

I waited…but she offered nothing more. What kind of freaking answer was that? I forced a laugh. "Well, that was a non-answer," I said.

"It's a perfect and complete response," she shot back, in that all-knowing tone of voice that braced my spine.

Thus started a fight that lasted through dinner. She was angry that I didn't accept her answer; I was angry because it wasn't one. We were each still fuming and defending our respective turfs when we returned home. She immediately disappeared into the barn, not to be seen again until morning.

Her "I told her nothing that I haven't told you already" continued to echo in my head long into the night. No matter which way I turned the lens, I saw her tight response as unacceptable. At the same time, I was aware that I had failed to hold my irritation in check. My tone had not been very conducive to productive conversation—again. Shame on me. I thought I knew better by now.

Okay, what could I have done differently? "I could have laughed, said that it didn't answer my question, and asked her another one to clarify it," I wrote in my journal. "There are two sides to every story and I didn't even try to understand hers." The discussion could have been so easy. Why did I get offended instead? Why did I take it so personally? She wasn't taking responsibility for her own stuff, but neither was I. Before I turned out the light, I jotted a final thought: "I wonder if I'll ever grow up..."

Saturday was one of those perfect spring days. The sky was cloudless, a light breeze was blowing in from the west, and the temperature hovered at a comfortable 75 degrees. I came downstairs that morning to find Kelly in the kitchen making Sarah and her sleep-over guest breakfast. She asked how I was and if I was holding onto last night's fight. I said no, I felt great. It was true. I was calm, something I hadn't felt for quite a long time.

According to my journal, Kelly and I dropped Sarah and her friend at a late morning movie, and then returned home and played cards upstairs on the floor of my room. Only later would I notice that I was now referring to this huge, newly-constructed suite as "my room." Kelly had separated to the point that I no longer regarded it as hers ... or ours.

We had a nice time playing gin rummy. There was no stress, no triggers, no anger—until she said, "You're shuffling the cards too fast." Huh? How does one shuffle cards too fast? She also commented that I dealt the cards with way too much intensity, then quick-covered with, "But those are my issues." Her tone made the hairs stand on the back of my neck. So did her repeated expressions of irritation about the way I shuffled and dealt. I was proud of myself when I didn't react with my usual anger. Instead, I spent the rest of the game shuffling and dealing in an exaggerated, super slow motion, with a big goofy smile on my face. I was learning.

Late that afternoon, the entire family went to Peddler's Village to hear Alex and his middle school choir sing in an outdoor concert. The Peddler's Village shopping complex, with its 46 shops, broad expanses of lawn and creative landscaping, is one of Buck's County top tourist attractions. As we walked from the car to the concert, Kelly said, "Let's try and hold hands. I don't want to, but we need to." That magnanimous "we" jostled a trigger. Was I supposed to think what a wonderful gesture it was? I held back, said nothing, and we walked the rest of the way hand in hand.

Sitting on the lawn waiting for the concert, Kelly put her head on my shoulder for a few brief seconds. A little later, she put her hand on my back, ever so briefly. After eight months of no physical contact, eight months of being told repeatedly, "I'm not in love with you," eight months of pure hell, I melted. Her mere touch excited me and instantly moved me to a place of optimism about a total reconciliation. She had just made her first effort, no matter how small.

While waiting for Alex after the show, Kelly said that she'd decided to commit to "the relationship." But to do that, she continued, she needed to talk with Scott – both to make herself "feel better" and to put the electrician behind her once and for all. She claimed that she'd never had "closure" with him.

In hindsight I see that I could have latched on to her pain, her integrity at having asked my permission, her move in my direction.

But instead, I fumed. How could she be so selfish, self-absorbed and arrogant? Had she no regard for how I felt? "All these months later, you're still dangling Scott in my face?" I demanded. In response, she trotted out her usual self-righteous mantra: "I'm just being honest."

As I write this almost two years later, I still remember vividly the crushing pain I felt as she spoke of "closure." But what I wrote in my journal was something quite different.

> Despite her wanting to 'have closure' with Scott, I still can't get past how much I love her. I look at her and just plain melt...no matter how bad it gets. I steal sideways glances at her at any chance. I watch her walk, hungrily cataloguing her beautiful body, so graceful and petite. My feelings for her are electric.

> I just want to be with her, hold her. It's not need, but rather my depth of feeling for her and my tactile nature. She's down to 106 pounds – the weight she married me at. God, I want to touch her so badly ... it aches to the core of my soul. Figuratively speaking, I don't think she knows I exist. My self respect must be at zero.

Janet had been pushing Kelly and me to go away together, just the two of us. She thought that a vacation, free of daily responsibilities and routines, would be healthy. She said it might help Kelly come closer to understanding what she really felt about me, about us, about herself. Janet also hoped it would help me to see Kelly with gratitude and understanding, rather than anger or resentment. Kelly, who'd resisted, saying she was "too scared," finally relented, albeit with hesitation, to spending a week on the Jersey shore.

God love Gatha, who agreed to stay with my kids for that week. I've known Gatha all my life. When I was eleven months old, she came to live with my family in Westport, and stayed for the next 20 years, leaving only after my kid sister went off to college. Gatha played such an important role in the lives of my siblings and me, helping to shape our formative years. She was another parent, the voice of reason, Mother Earth. She remains an integral part of the Lewis family. Now, she would play a vital role in my survival and recovery. And she would do it without question or hesitation, and with a depth of love that is magnificent. I know of nobody else who has the capacity to love so unconditionally. Suffice it to say, if everyone had just one Gatha in his or her life, this world would be a much more beautiful, caring place.

Small wonder, then, that my three kids adore Gatha as my siblings and I do. And just as my parents were once able to leave on periodic trips with total peace of mind, so were Kelly and I. Gatha's unconditional love for both Kelly and me was the nicest bon voyage present anyone could have given us as we headed out the door.

We left on a Friday afternoon in mid-May right after closing on a refinanced 30-year mortgage. I thought it more than a coincidence that in the midst of our chaos we were signing onto something so long-term. I translated that new mortgage to mean "reconciliation." I had such high hopes that the trip would move us forward and out of the agonizing rut we were in.

Our emotions were raw and on guard as we got in the car. I was grateful we were going; Kelly was terrified. We had no plans, no reservations. But it was pre-Memorial Day, so we assumed there would be plenty of vacancies. Conversation out to the shore was quiet and tentative. We found a bed & breakfast in Avon-by-the-Sea and, given our tight budget, took the most economical room. Though tiny, the room had a slanted roof and an inviting window seat. We unpacked quickly, and then headed out to a seafood restaurant.

After placing our order, I began to tell Kelly what I was learning through therapy and serious self-examination. I guess I got pretty animated. I came forward in my chair and leaned toward her across the table. Abruptly, she reared back in panic. Her reaction confused me. I had never *ever* been a physical threat to her. Feeling on safe ground, I apologized, explaining that I was just feeling enthusiastic about what I was learning and didn't mean to scare her. She retorted that this was typical of our 20 years together—I was focused on myself again, leaving her nowhere to go but into neutral territory to wait it out. The more I tried to explain, the worse it got. Out came her mantras: "I don't want to do this anymore." "I'm not strong enough to handle your energy." "We just miss." "I feel invisible around you."

I felt crushed, belittled, confused. For years, she'd complained that I'd never opened up to her. She decried that she didn't know who I was. Now, I was spilling my guts about lessons learned during her disconnection. How much more vulnerable and open could I be? Yet I found myself begging for forgiveness—not a very strong position to be in with a disconnected wife who says she wants an alpha male.

Later that night as she curled up alone on the window seat and went to sleep, I felt the sting of my fear of losing her. In my journal, I wrote:

> Are we on our last legs together? Is this trip going to signal the end?...She doesn't know if she feels anything for me – so she hides behind her perfect world of psycho-babble. She says I can't see past myself? I hate this situation and I don't agree with her logic which only serves to assuage her own guilt.

Then, with the aid of a little pill, I fell asleep feeling sad and more than a little panicked.

The next morning, everything changed. We found a wonderful new B&B, just off the beach in the cute oceanfront town of Belmar. Our mini-suite had a sun room that overlooked Silver Lake on one side and the ocean on another. The change of venue lifted our moods. We took long walks on the beach, read books, played cards and Scrabble, perused the downtown shops, napped. We also drank a lot of vodka and grapefruit juice. There was no physical contact, but the iceberg that separated us appeared to be melting, at least to me.

Two days later during one of our frequent walks along the beach, Kelly said her feet hurt and commented how much she'd like them rubbed. Reflexology has always been a Lewis thing. Walk into my parents' house during a family gathering and you're bound to see people sitting on floors and couches, talking animatedly and rubbing each others feet. So it was more habit than calculation that prompted me to grab Kelly's foot and start rubbing later that afternoon, while she was on the phone talking with the kids.

I was working her other foot by the time she hung up. Out of the blue she blistered me. "Do you have any intention when you rub my feet? Do you even *try* to be sensitive to what I might want?" Quickly, I released her foot and apologized, too stunned to feel even anger. But once again, there I was apologizing for doing something thoughtful and what I thought was considerate and nice.

The next morning over breakfast at the local diner, I put my hand out to hold hers for a pre-breakfast prayer, a ritual we do with the kids at most meals, one that Kelly had introduced into our family life. I reached over without looking at her, which made it come off to her more as a command than an attentive request. She went postal. "You don't pay attention. You have no idea that I even exist, much less what I want." Angrily, she likened it to the previous evening's foot massage.

This time, despite her ugly tone, absence of appreciation and total lack of gentility, she finally got through. She was right. I wasn't paying attention.

My reading had acquainted me with the concept of *mindful attention*. I was well-aware that this was something not integrated into my circuitry. For decades, I'd lived in my own little world, seldom noticing what was going on around me. I'd missed so many things. Now, I was finally aware enough to understand what I *wasn't* doing. I was also aware of the negative impact it had on me and on others—especially Kelly—who'd been on the receiving end of my inattentiveness for 20 years.

It was the first bad habit I was able to face honestly and actually change because I wanted to.

That night things took a beautiful turn. We were trying to sleep but there was, for the first time in those long nine months, a sexual tension between us. (The mood was no doubt assisted by the couple in the next room, whom we could hear through the thin walls having raucous and copious sex.) I rolled into Kelly's arm and put my head on her shoulder. Quietly, I said, "I really want to touch you. I know how scared you are. But I promise not to overstep my boundary. Is that okay?" She lay silent and unmoving, neither affirming nor resisting.

What followed was one of the most incredible sensory experiences in our marriage—at least for me. My touching, which is all I did, unleashed her sexual tension and need (I thought). It was powerful, gentle, caring and completely and mutually in synch (again, so I thought.) As my hand moved slowly and gently, sensing every movement, every need, I aimed only to please. I wanted nothing in return. When it was over, her pain returned. She put her pajamas back on and cried deeply – not from a sense of joy, but from years of pain. All I could think to say was, "Thank you for trusting me. I know how hard that was for you."

Tersely, she answered, "My body betrayed me." That was followed with, "I couldn't feel your sexual energy at all" and "I feel only shame."

Her unexpected words and harsh, abrasive tone hit me like a cold slap in the face and put me on the defensive. "I didn't move in on you, so to speak, but stayed removed out of a deep and abiding respect. You've hurt me so much with your constant comments. 'Don't touch me.' 'I'm not in love with you and may never have been.' 'I can't kiss you and I don't know how to find my way back.' I respected your position and let the touching talk. How many times have you complained about how fast I move? That I 'go for the goods' too quickly? That I'm not even aware of you, just thinking about myself? How many times have you humiliated me in the most intimate parts of our relationship?"

"It was horrible," she said flatly. "Why didn't you sense my emotional demand and have intercourse with me? Your hand and fingers were all over me. Your mouth was on my breast." She was angry now. "So why didn't you just put your penis inside me?"

I sucked in my breath, dizzy with horror at what she'd just said. *Why?* "Because you wouldn't look at me or kiss me—and I had to respect that," I said. "How do you make love to the woman you love so deeply when she can't do either? Don't you think I've heard and respected your nine months of 'Don't touch me'? I'm not out to hurt you, Kelly. Given where you've been, I thought you were taking a tremendous risk letting happen what just happened. I had such admiration for the size of the step you took. If you wanted more, then do what you keep telling *me* to do: use direct communication. *Ask for what you want.* How many damn times have you said that to *me*? Please, for once in your life, look at yourself and stop blaming me."

To say I was reeling is an understatement. Here, I thought we'd just had a breakthrough; there'd been such joy in the moment for me. Then, to hear, "My body betrayed me," and that I hadn't been mindful? I held the pain at bay, but not for long. The next evening, the last of our trip, I told Kelly that I was melting down (direct communication). I left the sun room without taking it out on her (something new for me) and sat alone on the bed trying to calm myself. I skipped dinner, took a sleeping pill and went to bed early.

When I awoke at 2:30 a.m., I dressed and went for a drive. I sat on the beach for a while, then went looking for an all-night diner. I struggled against the deep sadness and pain that I felt enveloping me, but it didn't work.

* * *

A little after 6:00 a.m., Kelly and I packed up. We decided to stop by the beach one last time on our way out of town. As we sat in the car watching the sun rise over the ocean, I tried to express the pain and anguish I felt from her rejection. Big mistake. She wanted to know why I wasn't more concerned about her feelings of shame. Why was I making it all about me?

It had required a tremendous effort the previous evening to walk away and not inflict my hurt, anger or blame on her. But after what had happened two nights earlier—not to mention nine anguishing months of rejection—her comment was like a match to a tinder box. She didn't want a loving spouse or a communicative mate; she wanted a cross between a mind reader and a punching bag. I couldn't hold back any longer. I lost it. And this time, I made no effort to spare her anything.

"Damn you! You blame me for everything. You tell me I'm not aware, I don't understand you, I'm insensitive to your needs. I could go on for hours with your little colloquialisms that hurt me so much over and over again. Here I was so sensitive to what you were experiencing and being completely respectful of where you were emotionally and all you can say is that I was making it all about me? How dare you, you selfish bitch! How fucking dare you!"

On and on I went, spitting out my rage with machine gun efficiency. My wife of 20 years had rejected me, and I was finally having my day in court. I'm not sure Kelly ever recovered from my outburst. I'm not sure I ever forgave her for her rejection.

Kelly's response to my outburst was silence. We drove home that way; Kelly curled up in the front seat facing the door, her back conspicuously to me.

And still, she was more beautiful to me than ever.

7. 25TH REUNION

Three events helped kick-start my long climb out of the dark depths. The first was the acquisition of my motorcycle license. The motorcycle safety course involved two evening classroom sessions, followed by a written exam. Next came two excruciatingly cold weekend sessions of riding instruction, then the driving test. Despite the fact that I couldn't execute figure eights to save my life, I now had a motorcycle license. The real question was whether I could survive on the open road.

Until now, my entire investment into this new hobby was $7 for the licensing fee. The DOT class had been free and Russ had extras of everything to lend me: helmet, leather jacket, gloves, even a motorcycle. I was ready—and I was scared shitless.

Though I wasn't as excited as Russ the following Saturday when we took our first ride, I was certainly game. My lifetime of prohibition surrounding the sport, however, still weighed heavily on my mind. My first foray did nothing to ease that trepidation. Coming out of Russ's driveway, I punched the accelerator too hard and the bike slipped out from under me on excess sand left from winter plowing. The bike skidded one way, I another. Scraped and ego-bruised, I looked up at the sky and wondered what the hell I was doing. "Hey," Russ said, laughing, "that happened to me too!" Great...

The bike Russ lent me was an old beater he had bought off the internet. The new dents and dings I had just added to its frame enhanced the already battered look. Russ was thrilled. Me, I got back up, muttered several choice expletives, and tried again.

I've never looked back.

* * *

The other two events coincided: my 25th college reunion and the reawakening of my friendship with an old high school girlfriend, whom I'll call Laila.

The reunion, scheduled for the end of May, raised plenty of trepidations. I didn't feel older, I certainly didn't feel wiser, and I had a hard time wrapping my mind around the idea that a quarter century had passed since graduation. It seemed way too recent that I was writing my senior thesis and trying to figure out what to do with the rest of my life. Now, here I was, 25 years later, *still* trying to figure out what to do with the rest of my life.

You're probably snickering at the thought of a bunch of middle-aged fogies getting together to drink beer and reminisce about *the good old days*. You gotta understand: Princeton does Reunions like no other institution in the world. Some 12,000 people, decked out in whimsical black and orange costumes, descend for a three-day party that involves music, dancing, shmoozy meals and, all right, plenty of brewsky. The annual highlight is the P-rade, which a decades-old article I found on Princeton's web site describes aptly:

> "Imagine a human behaviorist from another culture making his or her way through the wilds of central New Jersey to emerge onto campus on the morning of the event. What would he or she make of this bizarre ritual? Imagine if you will:
>
> An extremely old man — unmistakably the village elder — leads the members of his tribe, all dressed in variations of a highly symbolic uniform. Clearly, they worship the tiger. Groups of the celebrants

carry pictorial representations that are identifiable (in some instances, at least) as themselves when younger, seemingly inviting
comparison. This is a practice seen in no other society on earth.
Other members of the tribe carry placards emblazoned with cryptic
messages that elicit hoots and cheers from the watchers. One tribe
member — perhaps an outcast of sorts — passes by the parade on-
lookers on his hands. There is much repeating of talismanic words,
a kind of a guttural chant that sounds almost like "Sis-sis-sis-boom-
boom-boom-bah." A plea to some fearsome god, no doubt."

In short, Reunions promised just the sort of distraction I
needed. Yet I wasn't going to go. For one thing, there was the
money pressure. My job reduction, combined with the dead economy, had reduced my income by almost 40%. Despite some pretty
good savings, our cash flow was horrendous. I'd never done very
well with money pressure, so, though I lived only a forty five minutes drive from the campus, I sold myself on staying home to save
money. And, of course, I was such a basket case; I wasn't sure I
wanted classmates to see me in such a weakened state. It hurt to
feel so lost. It hurt to feel so worthless. It just plain hurt.

I'd always felt outclassed at Princeton. Most of my classmates
had come out of their respective high schools as Valedictorians
or something close to it. Me? I graduated 65th with SAT scores
about 150 points below my freshman class average. I only got into
the damn place because a professor, newly hired from Yale to start
a Theater and Dance program within the English department,
apparently thought I'd be an asset. I had no intention of being a
Theater and Dance major, but I'm a salesman, right? I delivered
an appropriately theatrical interview.

So there I was, a non-academic type at an Ivy League school,
competing with some of the brightest young minds in the country. Worse still, having fooled the professor about my academic

intentions, I felt like I was there under false pretenses. Throughout my four years at Princeton, I would continue to feel like a fraud—a feeling that would follow me into my adult work life.

Now, with my class's 25ᵗʰ reunion upon me, I received a questionnaire from a Reunion Yearbook committee that included a request that I write something. The idea was to share memories or a chronology of my last quarter-century or lessons learned along the way. "Just write what you'd think your classmates might like to hear from you or about you." The resulting essays were candid, hilarious and sometimes disturbing, comprising a remarkable portrait of the 1,185 men and women in the Class of 1978. Mine was an apt reflection of my state of mind—up to a point.

Princeton was quite an experience for me. I'm proud I made it through! But you've got to agree that it is definitely not a place for someone who isn't academically oriented, a category I put myself in. For the first three years I felt academically outclassed and terrorized that "someone" might find out. I finally gave up the self-deprecation senior year and actually had some fun - but it wasn't enough to keep me wondering ... even all of these 25 years later ... should I have gone somewhere else? Despite that, I am proud of myself for graduating and completing the experience.

These last 25 years have been fun. I've been married for almost 20 years and have 3 beautiful and accomplished children, all at different stages of "teenage hood". My oldest is almost 17 and a junior in high school. He is a good student, plays competitive hockey and lacrosse (two sports I never tried growing up which makes it all the more fun to watch), loves to snowboard and play guitar, and figures he'd like to move to Vermont and teach snowboarding before going to U of VT. Should be interesting to watch and see what actually happens! He's a cool kid with a great set of values.

Number 2 son is 15 and a high school freshman. He's my soul child, a gentle and sensitive young man. An accomplished pianist and computer jock, he has dabbled in the theater, loves to sing (belongs to 3 choirs) and is on the road to Eagle Scout. He too is an honor student and has talked about maybe going to Princeton. Trust me, based on what I said in the beginning of this write-up, I am not pushing the issue.

My baby is 10 and in 5th grade. She is 10 but going on 18. I'm sure you know the drill. God do they grow up fast. She is smart, creative and inured to the ways of men - something I assume she got by pushing back on her older brothers. She is my rose between the thorns and is nothing but a joy to behold and be around.

Kelly, my wife, has been through tremendous transformation since we married. I met her at IBM where she was a systems engineer. She hated it. Since then, she's tried creative writing, technical writing, artistry and motherhood. The last she does extraordinarily well. In the last 10 years, her interests expanded and opened up the world of counseling. This included completing her masters in counseling two years ago. She has been specializing in domestic violence and has now expanded out to all aspects of psychotherapy with additional focus on trauma and energy psychology. Her success and talents have become apparent as her practice grows.

And me, after 12 years with IBM, I went with a start up in 1990. I was the 8th employee. Today, we are publicly traded with around 500 people. Although the economy has hurt our valuation tremendously, we have not lost ground (although revenues continue to be flat at this writing) and are not burning cash. So, we just keep pushing and impatiently wait for the economy to turn.

Personally, I'm in a semi mid-life crisis ... but then who isn't? I keep asking, what is my value, to myself and to those around me? What have I really done to help change the world? Have I acted [on the Princeton motto] "In the nation's service"? Have I been truly present with what is happening right in front of me? It's a tough self-evaluation process. And I'm not crazy about some of the answers I'm finding. Change never came easily to me - so changing myself is a painful process. I am fortunate to have a loving and understanding wife to help me through the journey. And I am incredibly lucky to have 3 fabulous kids to love and who love me to help make this awakening so worthwhile.

What would I do differently if I had it to do all over again? I would learn to play the piano from an early age; I would invest far more wisely in the markets (this 'buy high, sell low' stuff is for the birds!); I'd be more aware of what is going on around me at every moment and not move so often in a fog; I'd appreciate everything and everyone around me instead of taking them for granted; and I probably wouldn't matriculate at Princeton but rather at a less rigorously academic institution. But none of that is possible or realistic. So I learn from my past, change what I can going forward and love the fact that I can forever say, "I graduated from Princeton University!" And I look forward to LIVING the next 25 years with health, happiness and a joy that is boundless and unparalleled. If I can do that, and I know I can, then I will be the luckiest person alive.

Though I submitted the essay, I still wasn't convinced I would attend the Reunion. I shared my reservations in a series of emails with Laila, an old high school friend from a deprived background (a rarity in Westport), with whom I'd reconnected two years earlier after a 25-year hiatus. I'll have more to say about Laila later, but for now, suffice it to say that Laila's re-entry into my life was a blessing. She was a roadmap to my past. A compass to my future. She was a gift from God.

The initial volley of emails about my dilemma began with a characteristic bit of wisdom from Laila:

I understand exactly how you feel. I felt like that almost every day in Westport...But think, Lewis. It seems logical to me that among the 12,000 (count 'em up, 12,000) alumni attending the reunion, you can't possibly be the only one suffering some kind of difficulty, whether financial or something equally dastardly, don't you think? Do you honestly think that graduating from an Ivy League college affords permanent, inalienable success? Don't the financially advantaged and educationally privileged have serious problems from time to time?

It also seems logical to me that of all of the doctors, lawyers, rocket scientists and Indian Chiefs there are in the United States, that more, collectively, graduated from "lesser" learning institutions and went on to be brilliant, successful professionals in their chosen field – with problems.

All of this is to say, the preachy long way, that you're being too hard on yourself. Go to the reunion and have a blast. You don't have to tell everybody everything (or anybody anything for that matter) and you can be a part of something special. It's only money (this, coming from someone who never had any.)

As for not being smart, you're kidding, right? You graduated from Princeton University and you're worried about being smart? There is always someone smarter, more successful – someone to envy; but if you look at them, examine their lives hard enough, they're either lying or have trade-off problems you don't want.

Sent: Monday, May 13, 6:17 PM

To: Laila

Yea, I need to go. I want to go. I'm just feeling sorry for myself. Besides, Newms is giving me the squeeze to come also. Remember her? Nancy Newman (lovingly known as Newms) is that brilliant, crazy, fun-loving, world-renown doctor down in your neck of the woods – that means somewhere below the Mason-Dixon line. There were many in college that just assumed she and I would get married some day even though we never really dated. (We tried it senior year to disastrous results). She too is facing an uncomfortable reunion for slightly different reasons. Her partner, Val, is obviously female (she's awesome, by the way). After a bunch of years keeping it out of the public eye, they have decided *not* to hide it at the 25th. Their 4-year-old daughter, Anna, is my loving, wonderful, talented, gorgeous godchild. (You don't sense a bias here, do you?!) Newms let me know that under no circumstance could I skip the reunion, because Anna would be there. A chance for me to see Anna is really enough to convince me. But she also let me know that I would be a cornerstone for her and Val. She really wants my presence for support. My love and respect for the two of them is so deep, how could I refuse?

So, last week I tracked down Ron, a classmate on the Reunion Committee, about letting me come just for the day on Saturday but at a greatly reduced price. It was embarrassing and I felt so small. But pressing on, I committed that I wouldn't bring any family members, could skip the big class dinner and that I didn't want the class costume which itself was a couple hundred bucks (yes, the class costume…). I told him the reality of my depressing financial situation. I felt compelled to explain that a year ago I had been riding high with a big net worth and no issues where money was concerned. But now I was in a place where I couldn't afford the cash flow of our newly renovated house much less the gas to get to campus for reunions. It was embarrassing if not downright humiliating to admit this to a classmate...

Ron was very understanding. He's apparently had a small handful of related requests from people in similar financial situations and said he'd get back to me with some sort of resolution or compromise. He went on to tell me that he himself was unemployed at the moment and could sympathize with my state of affairs. There's just one difference here and it strikes at the heart of my insecurity. Ron had a meteoric career at IBM and went on to become president of several software companies. His unemployment at the moment is no hardship and he is in no rush to find a job. He had recently sold his company, making what I can only assume to be a pile of money. Tack on to that the inevitable executive severance package to boot. His job loss is temporary while he evaluates lucrative offers to run other companies. His situation is no embarrassment; it's downright enviable.

I have to believe that a 25th reunion of this magnitude forces my whole class to reflect on what each of us has accomplished and aspire to achieve in the future. It should come at the most exuberant time in one's life and where the plate is overflowing with activity and opportunity. I just plain don't feel that.

This hits at the crux of my self-worth fear. My college peers have accomplished what I have not. There are so many successful lawyers, doctors and college professors. Two of my senior year roommates are presidents of their respective technology companies; my closest friend since graduating is considered the world's leading neuro-ophthalmologist; another is an Assistant US Attorney General. I could go on and on with the breadth and depth of the accomplishments of so many I read about while thumbing through the Reunion Yearbook. I feel anxious reading what so many others are doing and have done. I felt outclassed academically 25 years ago. Now I feel outclassed in career accomplishments and success.

Please don't mistake me for oozing a sense of complete failure. I'm not. I've made a very good living and a good life for me and my family. I've paid attention to the things that don't necessarily make headlines but nonetheless affect the lives of those around us. I've coached my kids' teams, sat on local not-for-profit boards, was president of my synagogue. I've been an attentive, loving and devoted father and (I thought) husband. But Kelly's disconnection even put that joy into question. She's thrown my whole life into question. And while I'm sorting it out, all I seem to be is miserable. I miss her so very much. She is emotionally so far away. It pervades everything I do, everything I think, everything I feel. Hell, she's my wife, my soul mate, my best friend — what would you expect?

Sent: Friday, May 16 3:23 PM

To: Laila

I'm going. Just got an email from Ron giving me dispensation to go under cover of night. He went on to say that if I tell anybody of the special deal the committee is giving me, they'll have to kill me. Actually, I really appreciate what they're doing for me and those few select others in the same financial boat. So I decided to face my trepidations and mailed off a check a few hours ago. It's just for the day on Saturday, but that's the big day anyway. Hey, it's the P-rade!

Yes, I said 'P-rade'; I assume it's short for the Princeton Alumni Parade or something like that. Insiders only know it as the "P-rade". Ask ANY Princetonian about it. If they don't burst immediately into a rousing chorus of the school alma mater, they'll just as enthusiastically smile and emit a heartfelt and contented sigh. Even the stiffest of the stiff alumnae transform into carefree children at play when marching in the P-rade. I remember watching Ralph Nader march in the P-rade at his 25th. Even HE was transformed into a smiling, happy youngster for an afternoon. It has that effect on all of us!

The P-rade is just that – a big parade. It's a choreographed march across campus. Alumni, friends and family line the campus parade route and the cheering, screaming and outright appreciation is uproarious and deliciously fun.

Despite how ridiculous it sounds to those who have never experienced one, the annual P-rade is truly an amazing sight and experience. Even for us turkeys who did nothing but struggle through our undergraduate years, the P-rade still elicits that pride of being part of the Princeton family. Remember the class costume I referred to a while back? Well, this is where it fits in...Trust me when I say that few class decisions prove to be more emotionally debated and controversial than the design of the 25th Reunion class jacket...So, down in the part of my being that is proud to say that I graduated from Princeton University, there is more than a small degree of sadness about not getting my own personal 25th Reunion class costume to march in. Dumb as it sounds, having my 25th reunion blazer would mean a lot to me...

Laila, I'm exhausted just telling you about it. I guess I am excited to be going, if only for the day. What hurts is that it should be a time of personal pride, a time to show off one's family. I can't afford to bring the kids, and my wife doesn't like me (herself?) very much right now. So where's the real joy? That's the bottom line. It's just tough approaching reunions feeling so fragile.

Sent: Saturday May 17   11:13 AM
To: Lewis, Jonathan
I'm going to be blunt: This one event seems to exemplify the center of your ego. Believe me, I can understand your feelings. Someone gave me the most enlightening piece of information many years ago, as I sat across from him behind his huge, expensive desk, sobbing hysterically because I thought my professional life was over – that I would be reviled in my industry and would be forced to leave it for the anonymity of, say, waitressing, out of the sheer humiliation of it all. He simply said this, "They aren't thinking about

you." I was damned near insulted until I realized how totally liberating this one fact was.

I can sense your agony over this, Jonathan, but no one is thinking about you. Sobering, huh? We all want to think we're more important to those acquaintances around us than we really are. They have their own issues, families, failures and problems to think about. They really aren't thinking about yours. I can almost guarantee that of the 12,000 who attend the reunion, not one will be aware of your difficulties unless you tell them, and those won't be nearly as concerned about you as you think they will. Except Nancy, Val and Anna who love you regardless, right? I have no alternative but to be cliché here - - isn't that what counts? If you get stuck in your own fears, look at little Anna. She'll bring you around.

We do this to ourselves. We drive ourselves crazy with comparing ourselves to "everyone else." Refer back to my first email. Do you think you're the only one out of 12,000 that fell on his/her ass? Aside from that, you'll get back up. One way or another, you'll get back up.

Sent: Sunday, June 1 2:14 AM
To: Laila

I went! After all of the wasted angst of fear and concern over social embarrassment and humiliation, I went! And it was so gratifying. Thank you for that extra kick in the pants – I can't believe I almost didn't go. What a grand day it turned out to be. What a fine night.

It's late (early?) and I need to sleep. But I couldn't rest without at least telling you the day was a success and not the grand disgrace previously assumed. Thanks for the shove.

Good night! I think I will actually sleep well.

The next morning, there was a shift in her tone and my response to it.

Picture this: I'm sitting here booting up the computer in my tattered blue bathrobe, wearing my favorite fuzzy old slippers, hair all askew and in dire need of a shower. It's a lovely Georgia morning (meaning the humidity has only reached 92% and the temperature hasn't crossed 100 yet). I have super-sized cup of coffee #2 by my side faithfully propping me up and slowly easing that Sunday morning desire to crawl back into bed and sleep the day away. Tom is long gone, off to feed his Sunday morning golf addiction. The house is deliciously quiet save for the hum of the computer and my bird chirping away in the living room. I log onto email hoping, hoping, hoping for news from the North Country to spice up my day. I see that glorious alert "You have (1) new message". My dream's come true, it's from you! The 'Subject' line reads "25th Reunion". YES, I think, my morning is made – he's going to tell me all about it. I eagerly open the new message anticipating a long, descriptive narrative about your trip back down memory lane. I imagine the juicy details soon to grace my computer screen. I shiver with visions of tantalizing descriptions about your step back into the past. My breath quickens as I eagerly anticipate you teasing me with redoubled joy about feeling so young because all of your classmates have aged so much less gracefully than you. I tingle all over as you describe the patch-work of balding heads, pot bellies and faces full of wrinkles encountered. How could they have gotten so old, I expect you to query.

So what do I get? "It was a fine night".

Damn you, Lewis. Get your cute ass back to the keyboard and talk to me. This is totally unaccept-able. You've absolutely doused my morning in ice water. You've left me totally unsatisfied. How can you do that to a woman in such need? I'm going back to bed – alone and unfulfilled.

Sent: Sunday, June 1 3:24 PM
To: Laila

I'm horrified! How could I leave such a lovely, desir-able woman so displeased and so unsatisfied? To recover from this abhorrent aberration, I shall slowly weave you into my web of reunion delight. Sit back, relax, breathe slowly and deeply. Feel the tingling sensa-tions as I delicately run my fingertips across this ever sensitive keyboard. We'll take it nice and slow. Can you feel the tension rising? How long can you stand it without exploding? You asked for it, you got it. This might take some time, so enjoy the ride...

It all started on a drizzly, dank Saturday morning (uh, yesterday). I dragged my aching back out of bed and onto the floor. While stretching and going through my morning yoga routine, doubts about going to the reunion preoccupied me. By the time I got into the shower 30 minutes later, I was damn near sure that I wouldn't go at all. Thoughts of showing up without a class outfit, without my wife, sans kids, a stalled career going in the wrong direction and feeling like the kiss of death, convinced me that everyone would see through this hollow, vacant man. Through this hour of extreme vacillation, it was only the prospect of disappointing Nancy and Anna that propelled me forward. They had asked for my support. We could support each other.

I have no memory of driving to campus. It's just not anywhere to be found in the filing cabinets of my brain. If someone told me I had been teleported over by aliens from a distant planet, I might just believe them so big is the blank. That alone should explain my frame of mind when I actually pulled into the parking lot at the base of the campus. And then the lights came on.

It was the strangest thing. Drizzle was still falling intermittently when I got out of the car. It was also apparent that the lousy weather wasn't going to clear so quickly if at all. So the decision *not* to carry an umbrella established some kind of emotional beach-head in my psyche. Weather be damned. If I'm gonna' get wet, I'm gonna' get wet. I wasn't going to schlep around an umbrella all day. And then came my "Wizard of Oz" moment. It was like Dorothy stepping out of the fallen house in Munchkin Land – and into a world of color.

I went on to tell Laila how I slammed the car door and stood for a second with my eyes closed, gathering my resolve. I took a deep breath and, with a long slow exhalation, turned toward campus. Then, it happened. Exactly what "it" is I don't know; I just know everything changed. I looked across the sea of cars and up the hill toward the main part of the university grounds and all of the jitters, doubts, brooding and dark trepidations that almost kept me away vanished. I was back at school. I was home.

So many memories flooded my mind as I walked up campus toward the 25th Reunion tent. There was 17 Spelman, my extremely cool senior year dorm apartment. And Pyne Hall, where I lived and struggled through my freshman year. There were the tennis courts and the hill we had so much fun on senior year during the great blizzard of January '78. Classes had been cancelled, so we stole trays from the Commons dining hall to use as sleds. No one got mad at us as would have been the norm; in fact some of the usually dour administrators joined in the fun.

My god, I thought, taking in the landscape that I'd virtually ignored as a student, just look at how incredibly beautiful this campus is. Even in the dank haze of the rainy morning, everything looked so alive. The colors were so vivid. I had never associated the school with color before, yet there it was, clear as day. I could feel my adrenaline surging. Each step I took got lighter. My cloud of anxiety was lifting and a smile was bubbling up from my inner depths.

"Jonathan, Jonathan!" a voice pierced my reverie.

It took me a second to re-acclimate. Oh my god! "Lindsey, is that really you?"

"Uh huh. It is *so* good to see you," she exclaimed as we hugged and danced around like little kids. (This was a scenario that would play itself out all day long: recognize someone, let out a yelp of greeting, then hop up and down and around as you hugged. Sometimes it's good not acting like an adult!) Lindsey hadn't changed a bit. Her eyes still sparkled like they always had. Her energy was palpable. Except for a little gray around the edges, she looked absolutely the same. "I got to tell you, Lewis," she said as we disentangled, "your write-up in the yearbook really touched me."

I laughed, surprised. "You read it? I mean, there were over a thousand essays. Don't tell me you read the book cover to cover?"

113

"Yeah, pretty much. Well, I had the long trip from the coast to get here so I had time to read it on the plane. It certainly made the trip go by quickly. And I'm serious, your essay really stood out, really hit a chord. I mean, did you truly feel like that back then?"

"I did."

"It's funny, but I felt a lot like that too," she said. "I felt intimidated and unworthy being here. I thought it was only me and my own insecurities, so I buried it where no one else could see it. It was obvious from your write-up how painful it was for you. I hate to revel in your pain, but it's nice to know that I wasn't the only one." I gave her what must have been a strange look. "What?" she asked.

"Well, I'm stunned you read and remembered what I wrote. So thank you for that. I think I'm flattered. But my thank you goes so much further than that. I mean, you seemed so academically comfortable. It never would have occurred to me that you, of all people, would have been unsettled here."

"Look who's talking," she replied. "You were the most relaxed, confident guy around. Your discomfort never would have occurred to me either!"

We exchanged a few more pleasantries and agreed to seek each other out during the day. Then, she pointed me in the direction of the 25th Reunion tent and we parted company. It turns out I didn't see her the rest of the day, but it didn't matter. She had unknowingly started a ball rolling for me. It would pick up speed as the day progressed.

I eventually found the tent and followed the signs into one of the nearby buildings to register. Within the general area of this highly attended reunion tent, a person couldn't make it more than two or three feet in any direction without bumping into a memory—usually in the form of a long-since forgotten classmate. But it was like the clock had stood still. Faces and names flooded my brain. Images of days gone by surfaced. We all became teenagers again. Hey, there's Mike! We rowed crew together freshman and sophomore years. And there's Sally, one of the surprisingly few who smoked cigarettes. Oh look, that's Tom. Freshman year he streaked Holder quad and the surrounding dorms with his girl-friend, Jean, in the dead of winter. (This to the rousing approval of a couple hundred appreciative classmates.) I wonder if Jean's here!

It went on like this all day. I found Nancy, Anna and Val pretty quickly, to our mutual delight. We laughed and carried on through-out the rest of the day like we were part of Anna's playgroup - a bunch of happy four year olds. As we greeted long-lost classmates and friends, we never strayed very far apart, supplying each other with love and a security blanket. I felt so good watching Nancy, and the strength with which she was handling her situation. She stood tall (which is tough for a woman who maybe hits 5 feet on a good day) as she introduced Val around. Val of course was a rock. She's always been calm, steady, strong, brilliant and totally at ease with herself. But Newms, like me, is far more emotionally driven. She knew heads were turning but pressed on. If she was nervous, and I'm sure she was, it never showed.

Watching her in action was cathartic. Look at her, I thought. She was and is Superwoman. She won a Marshall scholarship in Art History, and was our Pyne Prize winner (huge academic recogni-tion). She was also president of the crazy Princeton band; performed with me in the musical-comedy Triangle Club; played a wicked game of co-ed volleyball; and had spirit to spare. After returning from her two-year Marshall scholarship in England, she attended Harvard Medical School, where she again graduated top of her class. She was elected to Princeton's Board of Trustees, a position she held for 14 years. And here she is, setting herself free by simply staying with the truth, a truth she didn't even know existed until she met Val. What an amazing human being. What a wakeup call for me.

Newms wasn't the only person who helped me gain some perspective. With my entire being so caught up in my marital drama, I hadn't stopped to think that maybe I wasn't the only person in the world who'd felt the sting of a love lost. My close friend Lucas was the first of several people that day to remind me that love fails, marriages crumble, yet life goes on.

Luke and I had hung out a lot during our undergraduate years. When he married soon after graduation, his wedding was a big fancy Princeton affair, orchestrated by his fiancé, who was a few classes behind us and a native New York City socialite from the posh Upper East Side. Luke and I drifted apart after the wedding—a combination of physical distance and his wife, who I came to learn felt threatened by our friendship. To this day I still have no idea why. I'd missed him across the years.

Now, his story quickly emerged. Two and half years ago, 20 years and three kids into their marriage, his wife grew bored with being a stay-at-home mom. She unsuccessfully tried her hand at selling real estate, and was flailing for something new to do when a neighborhood friend, who was in the throes of a divorce, invited her to come on a 10-day buying trip to the Orient. This woman, who ran a Tupperware-type business selling Asian art and trinkets at home parties, made such trips twice a year to replenish her inventory. Luke, thinking such a trip might be just the thing to shake his wife out of her funk, encouraged her to go.

She went and, in effect, never returned. Her homecoming announcement was that she was leaving Luke—for the female traveling companion/neighbor.

There was such pain on Luke's face as he described what happened next. He loved his wife and didn't have a clue that anything had been wrong or off-kilter in his marriage. He was certainly not aware that she was unhappy or discontent in their relationship. For the next year, he struggled to save his marriage. He dragged his wife to counseling. He begged, he pleaded. (Does this sound familiar?) But she wouldn't budge. In the end, he saw no choice but to give up trying to win her back. His divorce had only recently gone final, the assets had been split up and each had completed buying substantially smaller homes. The kids were now shuttling back and forth between Luke and his ex. His oldest child, a college freshman, was so angry that he'd stopped talking to his mother. The parallel was a little eerie - for a short period of time, my son Mike similarly stopped talking to his mother.

I pressed Luke on how he survived the ordeal. How was he able to get out of bed each morning during the worst of it? He said that work and his kids saved him. As president of the U.S. operation of a European-based software company, a job that he loved, Luke was traveling almost full-time. Being out of town a lot, he said, was essential to his sanity. Seeing his wife was just too damn painful. When he was home, he immersed himself in activities with his kids. The combination of the travel and the kids helped him through the worst of the abandonment.

Luke told me that he was now dating. He said it was weird being back in a world he had left so long ago and never thought he'd re-enter. "But here I am," he said, with a weary smile. Though the pain of his divorce was ebbing, it still hit him in waves. "The waves can be unbearable," he said. "But they get easier to handle as time goes on."

Then, he asked how Kelly was doing. I told him. I was honest about the situation and didn't try to hide anything. That alone surprised me, but my candor didn't make me uncomfortable. He listened carefully. There were no surprised reactions, just nods of comprehension. If anyone could understand my situation and pain, I guess it was Luke. When I finished, he gave me a hug and expressed his sympathy for the ordeal that I was going through. He also mused how difficult it must be to be caught in Never Never Land.

"Huh?"

"At least with me," he said, "when I finally faced it, I knew my marriage was over and had no choice but to move on. It's kind of like death; you just have to accept it because you can't change it. There was no hope of reconciliation—at least not after that first year of trying. But you, you don't know if Kelly is coming or going, and it sounds like she doesn't either. So you're stuck. You can't get on with your life because you love her and don't want to give up on your marriage. She doesn't like what was, but isn't walking away from you, either. She doesn't know how she feels, except she's not in love with you right now. She's got you pinned. You don't want to move on, but you can't go back. Never Never Land."

He probed to see what I was thinking, what I was doing to heal from the situation, what responsibilities I was taking for causing this sad state of affairs.

"Damn," I snorted. "You sound like my therapist."

"Absolutely," he responded. "If I learned nothing else from my divorce and all the therapy to get there, it's that I had to take responsibility for my own life and for my role in the break up. Her leaving for another woman was about her, not about me. Yes, I was a catalyst. But I was an effect, not the cause. Her shit is her shit, not mine. I just took it so personally, as any normal human would do in a situation of this kind. The pain of abandonment, loss and betrayal can't be minimized. When you love someone, it's hard to stand far enough back to see that it's really not about you."

"Sounds so clinical," I said.

"I only present it that way because I'm *still* trying to accept it. I can speak the words, but I certainly don't feel them all the time. But trust me, it does get easier with time—well, at least once you make a decision."

Though I listened attentively to Lucas, trying hard to benefit from his hard-won wisdom, I didn't really have a clue what he was talking about. How could Kelly's shit be her shit, and not mine? My life was so entangled with hers that the idea that her happiness might be unconnected to me was no more conceivable than the possibility that my happiness was unconnected to her. Try as I might, I just couldn't see it. As I wrote in this lengthy email to Laila:

```
Luke was pretty passionate, I gotta give him that.
The bastard also made me think about me and focusing
on my own role in this predicament, and not wasting
so much time and anger blaming Kelly. All I can do is
look at myself. The only thing I can change is myself.
It sounds so simple. I've heard it in therapy too many
times and [aren't] buying it.
```

I then shared with Laila some of the other conversations I'd had beneath the 25th Reunion tent. Now that I'd opened up and permitted myself to talk about my struggling marriage, it was amazing what people were willing to share in return. Among the most chilling stories was the one told by Wendy, an acquaintance from my Pyne Hall days, about the demise of her own 20-year marriage. (What *is* it about that number?) I guess I say chilling because I heard so many parallels between her marriage and mine, including that, like Kelly, she'd become a therapist in her middle years. Now divorced, Wendy expertly grilled me about the details of my own situation, then said, "You're unlucky, Jonathan."

"Why?"

"You had no traumas in your childhood, no experiences to toughen you. How could you possibly know how to deal with it now that one has hit? And this one's not just your average rainy day trauma; it's a monsoon. You have no reference point. How do you expect to deal with something so overwhelming when you have no tools to fall back on? How can you logically recover from it so you can move forward, when your love and emotions are so heavily invested? The good news is that you were very well protected growing up. The bad news is that you were very well protected growing up. Understand?"

I didn't. Not really. But apparently Laila did.

"When you're in crisis," she emailed me back, "it's hard to view any situation clearly. And Baby, you're in a crisis of unspeakable proportions."

Despite Laila, Luke and Wendy's best efforts, and several other peoples as well that day in Princeton, I still didn't "get" what any of them was trying to tell me. I was still too cloudy and confused to comprehend the scope of the catastrophe that had befallen me. All I could see was that somehow, some way, I had fucked up big time—and was not bouncing back nearly fast enough.

Amazing as it seems to me now, as I listened to my friends' stories it never once crossed my mind that what had happened to each of their marriages might happen to mine. Though Kelly had made that one vague allusion to divorce two months earlier, the possibility of an actual break-up had settled in neither my brain nor my heart. Kelly and I were having a bad patch, yes. But we loved each other; we wanted to remain together. We would get through this. I didn't doubt that, not even for a moment.

I could sell myself anything.

8. GROSS DIRECT COMMUNICATION MISCONDUCT

Reunions lifted my spirits. The next day, Kelly and I awoke around 7:00 and stayed in bed until 9:00. This had been one of those rare nights when she chose our bed over the barn, though she stressed, "Only because I sleep better." I think deep down I was hoping that going to Reunions without her might have thrown her a little. But looking back I have to believe it was just my wishful fantasy. Anyway, we talked of inconsequential things and even cuddled. Let me be more precise: I spooned around her. When she didn't pull away, I put my head on her shoulder. Being wrapped around her was electric for me. Slowly and gently, I ran my fingers across her belly. She didn't respond; then again, she didn't pull away. Hmm. Heart pounding, I extended the touching up to her ribs and down to her hips. It went no further than that. It was respectful.

Later, I asked if she was okay with what I had done. "You weren't looking at me," she fumed. "How can I feel anything? It's no different than it's always been."

Her words made me nauseous. Her tone of voice made me sick. All I could offer was a feeble, "My head was resting on your shoulder. How could I possibly look up at you from that position?"

At times like that, it was particularly hard to remember what Janet kept repeating in therapy: "Kelly needs you to acknowledge her emotional reality. And she needs you to do it without anger or condemnation. She's still terrified, scared of losing herself." Instead, I went into defense mode. I got hurt, so I got angry. I got angry, so I blamed her. I blamed her, so I got judgmental. I still couldn't see that my anger was my worst enemy—and that it was sinking my marriage. Because of my anger, I couldn't get past my own hurt and humiliation and sit quietly long enough to see the demons *she* was fighting.

I kept thinking about what Luke had said at Reunions: "It's not about you, it's not about you, it's not about you." But when I was hurting and angry, it was impossible to remember or feel that. I *did* take it personally. And I missed her so much. Even when she was right there, she was unreachable.

That night, we watched Barbara Walters interview Hillary Clinton. Remember, Bill was still in the White House at that time. After it was over, we started talking about the possibilities of a woman president and Bill Clinton as "First Man." Kelly said that we are still a patriarchal society, and that women at the local level aren't helped or heard at all. I countered that women have come far in the last 30 years, though not nearly far enough, and thought the momentum for change was there. She pushed back. The discussion was lively and interesting.

As we talked, Sarah came in with a draft of a family tree she was drawing for school. She was having design problems. Kelly suggested that she go outside and study a tree up close, a suggestion she'd apparently made earlier. When Sarah stomped out of the room, unhappy and irritated that she was not going to get further help, I asked Kelly if it might be a good idea for her to take Sarah to a tree and discuss what she sees; given my lack of artistic talent, I felt unqualified to do it. I added that she'd often verbalized how bad she felt about leaving Sarah alone so often. Wouldn't this be a great opportunity to spend time with her?

Kelly's response was pure battery acid. "Oh, what you're really saying is that we need to spend more time with her. It's not about the tree." Kelly then hissed at me that she was talking to her husband, trying to build a relationship. With that, she got up and stormed out of the room.

I sat stunned and confused on the couch. Okay, what did I do wrong *this* time? Kelly often worried about the amount of time Sarah was spending alone. She had commented more than several times that she, Kelly, should do some projects with Sarah to spend quality time with her. She had also been very vocal about *not* wanting to talk about our relationship (which, in fact, we weren't doing until she took the swipe).

I reconstructed the discussion, searching for what I could have done differently. In counseling, Janet often beat me up about coming from my head, not my heart. "What Kelly is begging for," she said, "is that you come from your heart." So, what would have been from the heart? "Oh Kelly, did you see how sad Sarah was? Let's put our discussion on hold so you can go spend time with her." That didn't feel heartfelt; it just felt stupid. Besides, my intention was exactly the same.

The next morning I dumped all of this on Laila in a phone conversation. I had to cut our dialogue short to dial in to a business conference call, but Laila didn't let me off the hook. Within minutes, her incoming missile set me straight.

Sent: Monday, June 9 9:07 AM

To: Lewis, Jonathan

Subject: Ouch

Actually, that is exactly what you should have said. Hey, Tom's a therapist too. I know exactly what you're talking about. Plus, I'm a woman so I can understand Kelly's need.

She wants you to acknowledge her. In this case, she wanted you to acknowledge that you were in conversation with her and explain *why* you were suggesting putting it on hold. It validates her, it says you're sensitive to your relationship with her and that each conversation with her is critically important to you. It says you aren't taking her for granted.

Wake up, Jonathan, she's not running away from you. She's just not running toward you the way you want her to. Give up the ego and give her what she wants. The only other two choices you got are to suffer (which you're doing very well, thank you) or to leave. It's really not so bad, you know. We women LIKE to be acknowledged once in a while.

"Give up the ego." How the hell does a natural born salesman give up his ego? It's his survival mechanism. Salesmen know how to take rejection; we know that rejection is just the first step of a negotiation. But my conversation with Kelly hadn't felt like a negotiation. It felt more like a door slamming in my face.

Plainly, I wasn't catching onto the lesson of "direct communication," one of Janet's favorite themes. Instead, the exchange with Kelly left me feeling like men and woman really do come from different planets. I seemed to be stuck in a repeating loop.

About three weeks later, that point was brought home again, only this time, the messenger was Tiffany Burton. Tiffany and I went to junior high, high school and Princeton together. I doubt we exchanged a dozen sentences in all those years. We'd met up again at the 25th Reunion, where I'd learned that Tiffany is now an established psychologist in Philadelphia and herself a recent divorcee. Like many of the conversations I had that day, ours ended with pledges to get together for lunch, blah, blah, blah. This time, though, I actually followed through and called her. I'm in and out of the City of Brotherly Love often; I thought lunch would be fun. Frankly, any social contact was a welcome respite from my misery.

We set a lunch date for Friday, the 13th —which probably should have been my first clue what a bad idea this was. Two days after our get-together, at which we discussed my marriage and she talked about her own marital break-up, she sent me an email. Thus started one of the most bizarre exchanges I've ever experienced, one that reinforced my sense that I was guilty of gross direct communication misconduct.

Sent: Sunday, June 15   10:49 AM

To: Lewis, Jonathan

Subject: thanks

Hi Jonathan, it's Tiffany. I just wanted to thank you for lunch and to tell you to hang in there. It's a long road, but as I told you, it sounds like you're doing all the right things for yourself, your wife and your kids, and all you can do is see how it plays itself out. As I have learned, there are so many things over which we have no control, and one of those things is about how another person feels about us and what they want. I admire your tenacity and willingness to ride the wave as far out as it will take you, as long as it doesn't damage your sense of what's important to you.

As you know, we're all far from perfect and don't always act with wisdom and vision. All we can do is move forward and try to make the next phase of life as full and as rich as possible.

Good luck with everything, and thanks again. It was good to see you again.

I responded immediately. I expressed my gratitude for her vote of confidence and thanked her for listening to my tale of woe. I then suggested that maybe we could get together for lunch again and agree *not* to talk about spouses/exes; it's bad enough she did it every day as part of her job. I went on to suggest that at the next lunch, I would ask most of the questions—meaning I would listen more than talk, something that hadn't happened the first time around. Exercising my best "direct communication" skills, I strove to let her know that there was so much more that I wanted to know about her. My email concluded:

Tiff, I hate to admit it, but since Junior High, I'd been completely intimidated by you - you were/are way smart, very beautiful, mysteriously quiet and outwardly sophisticated far beyond us mortal men, especially adolescent ones.

Now I'd just like to get to know you. It would be nice to take the mystery out of who you really are. And by not being intimidated anymore (that's the adult, self-confidence thing emerging ...) it will be nice to learn who you really are. I believe that beneath your quiet exterior lies the heart and courage of a lion.

I look forward to another lunch!

I was pretty proud of myself, I can tell you. I'd been open and honest. A regular Direct Communicator.

Right.

Four days later, I got this response:

Hi Jonathan,

I have some thoughts about what you wrote.

1. Thank you for the compliments about how I seemed, or how I was, but I'm actually not so mysterious. I was just a shy girl, quite introspective, and not at ease around boys. Princeton helped a lot with that.

2. I thought the purpose of our lunch *was* so that you could talk about your in-house separation and hear about my similar story and get some strength from that. So I expected to talk about that. Your life has turned upside down and it makes sense that you'd want to hear how others have coped.

3. I think you need to stay focused on what's going on there. Although I appreciate your wish to get to know me now, I think your energy and attention probably should stay with the therapy, marriage counseling, and so forth. I'm no one in that family drama, and you're one of the leading players. I'm just a distraction.

4. Due to our common history, growing up in Westport, going to Staples, and then to Princeton, I think we will always be friends. I always feel a special camaraderie with anyone who's lived a similar past. I expect that will always be there.

So, I don't think we should have any more lunches at present. Take good care of yourself and keep on working hard on everything you're trying to achieve. For your sake I pray your marriage works out and you can find peace in your home again.

Is my life and every encounter really this surreal?

Sent: Friday, June 20 8:18 AM

To: Tiffany_Burton@psych.com

Wow. I think something got misread here. My intention in requesting lunch with you again was strictly a social one. I enjoyed talking with you and would have loved to pursue other subjects of interest. You're an intriguing person that I sadly never got the chance to know. You would be anything but a distraction. The implication of #3 of your email, however, as well as the last paragraph infer you think I am looking for something more. I'm sorry if that was the signal I transmitted. As I said quite emotionally over lunch, my marriage means everything to me. Kelly's disconnection took me totally by surprise. My whole focus since then has been and is to repair it. There can be no emotional distractions in the process. I'm an old-world Jewish kid who takes marriage seriously. The thought of acting outside of it is foreign to my way of thinking.

Kelly knew I was having lunch with you. There were no secrets or subtext or hidden agendas. And I'm very sorry if it came across any other way.

That said, I respect your request and will abide by it. I do, however, think it's a shame. Friendships should be gender-irrelevant. I guess in your profession, however, you see so much that points otherwise...

Kelly and I will work our marriage out, one way or the other. It's what we both want - but we also both want it healthy - which it apparently wasn't. What a process.

```
    Thanks for the talk last week. Your insights were
helpful.
    Respectfully, Jonathan
```

Three weeks would go by before I heard from Tiffany again. Her response landed on my 47th birthday. Happy birthday to me …

```
    Hi Jonathan, In re-reading your original email, I
realized that I overreacted and would like to apolo-
gize. I've felt badly about it. I hope the next time we
run into each other, at a Staples or Princeton reunion,
it will be forgotten. Hope your situation is improving
and that you're enjoying the summer.
```

This time, I wanted to think my answer through more carefully. I'd apparently blundered once; I didn't want to do it again. So I consulted the Oracle: my sister, Jill. I figured her incisive mind, coupled with the fact that she vaguely knew Tiffany, would help pave the way for a clean response. Her insight was spectacular and allowed me to craft a response two days later without hesitation or concern.

```
    Tiffany, thank you. Needless to say, I was a bit
flustered by the whole interchange. Thus, I appreciate
all the more your email.
    In my dismay, I told my sister, Jill, (remember her?)
about our email exchange following the lunch. My purpose
was to see if I had done something - anything - that might
have led to your initial conclusion. Maybe I had given off
some kind of signal without knowing it. After a moment of
thought, she laughed and said: "I bet she doesn't have any
brothers." I asked why, not quite catching on. She said
that she's noticed very strongly over the years looking
```

at her close female friends that those who grew up with brothers, especially ones close in age, are constantly surrounded by their brother's friends (males). It is natural and normal to be comfortable around them growing up in this strictly social environment. She said that to this day about half of her good friends are men and that she has never had a concern/intimation about intimate possibilities or pressure from them. It would never even be considered that a man couldn't be just as good a (platonic) friend as a woman. However, she continued, her female friends who didn't grow up with brothers, invariably view *all* men as potential partners/threats depending on their relationship status at the time. The thought of men as just friends is, in fact, anathema to them. (I look at my ten closest friends today, six are men, four are women.)

Right or wrong, it was an interesting perspective. Anyway, I do appreciate your email. Thank you.

I never did hear from Tiffany again. That was okay.

* * *

Around this same time, Russ and Mary Ellen bought another house, this one earmarked as their retirement domicile. A gorgeous historic home, it sits on the scenic Delaware River. While fixing it up, they offered it to Kelly as a retreat. When she declared her intention to spend a weekend there, I fought back. How can you do that? I demanded. How can you abandon us? She went anyway. Though she was only nine miles away, this felt more momentous than her move across the driveway into the barn.

Bereft, I plowed into my journal. By now, I was starting to realize (largely through my growing email correspondence with

Laila) that there was something private and satisfying about writing, something that encouraged me to explore further. This was a big surprise for a guy who was accustomed to never using two sentences where one would suffice. ("Dear Mrs. Smith, Thank you for your lovely gift. Love, Jonathan.") Now, writing was fast becoming like a drug; I couldn't get enough.

> Kelly went off today to spend the weekend at the Reeds' new house on the river in Washington's Crossing. She called it "Alone Time." I'm actually glad that she's there. She is really in a place where she just needs quiet and introspection. I'm in her way. Isn't that a sad thing to say?
>
> I feel so boxed in. I'm not completely able to respond from my heart yet – but I'm working at it. You wouldn't know it being around Miss Perfect. Everything has to be just so or she goes off the deep end. Why do I get so irritated over it? Have I no self control?
>
> Yes, I know that I don't get *direct communication* yet – she knows that too, but without compassion or sympathy of any sort. I'm trying to change a lifelong habit of being indirect, not stating what I'm really thinking. It's hard. I still have anger, although it seems greatly reduced these days. Can't she get that my anger is really just my hurt of her humiliations and ejection of me – that surfaces as verbal irritation? She still jumps so ugly. And she hides behind her mantra, "I just can't take it anymore."
>
> I need to stop reacting. I am *so* sick of her high and mighty, "I'm so spiritual" attitude. If I hear her say one more time, "This is what God wants us to do; it's perfect," I'm going to scream. I can't stand her sitting in constant judgment, her lecturing, her condescending tone, her smug superior attitude.

Maybe this won't work out. Maybe she *should* just fucking leave.

My emotions are raging and it's out of control at times. It's not a violent anger; rather it's overwhelming frustration and the fear that comes with the loss of love. It is so hard to look inside myself and be honest … with me.

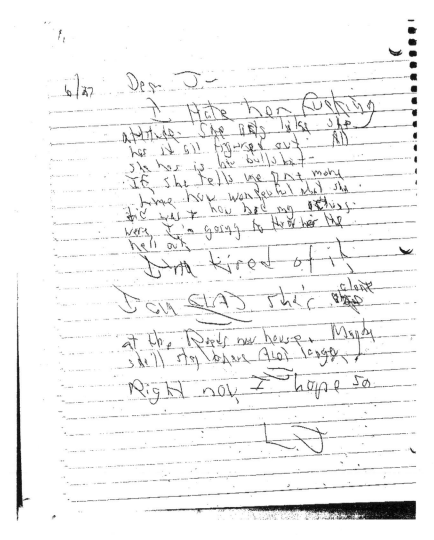

As the little boy in me makes evident, the agony of Kelly's rejection was not loosening its grip. I always felt stupid responding to the

Little J letters. But I didn't know who else to say this to. So, I wrote the little dude back, trying hard to be the sane, mature adult.

> Hey Little Guy,
>
> I feel your frustration. She's in such a vulnerable, confused place right now and we are sometimes a target. We have to remember to come from our hearts & not our emotional side. I know that I, like you, struggle mightily with it.
>
> I am learning to say what I feel at the moment an emotion surfaces. It can be hard sometimes because I'm still not always sure what I feel. You are allowed to feel all of your emotions – in fact you absolutely should. Please be sure you are honest with yourself about what the emotion is – because it is always about you, not anybody else. Your reactions are just that – yours. You choose how to receive it – and shouldn't ever take it personally. It's hard, but I know, with time, you can learn this fine skill. It will make your life so much less stressful and so much happier.
>
> I am here for you. Look to me if and when you need peace and tranquility and calm.
>
> Always Yours – Big J

A year into this crisis Kelly and I seemed to be no closer to building a new foundation for our marriage. Time had passed, but my shock and numbness had not. I wasn't sure *what* I believed any more. I had lost the cornerstone of my support system. I still felt completely victimized. I was helplessly plugged into a security system that no longer existed. I could see that I was Linus without his blanket—but the reality of my situation was still not sinking in.

Not, I might add, for lack of trying. At this point, my bedroom was a veritable library of books for the middle-aged man in crisis. I inhaled these volumes: self-help, psychology, religion, New Age, philosophy. I was convinced that if only I could find the right book, the right page, the right paragraph, the answers to my problems would become clear.

What you get out of a book, of course, has a lot to do with what you bring to the reading of it. Given my state of mind at the time, much of it seemed like psychobabble (translation: bullshit). The repetitive messages of "Stay Present," "Only you can make you happy," "Just sit with it," made me want to barf. It would take another year for those chestnuts to have any real meaning. In the meanwhile, one recurring refrain *did* strike me. *Have faith to let it go. Open your heart and your mind. Life is a good teacher and a good friend.* One way or another, they all seemed to offer the same message: Step boldly into the present moment—no matter how painful, frightening or uncertain—and have faith that a higher purpose is awaiting you. Only when your usual schemes fall apart [that was me, for sure] can you find sanity and open yourself up to the unconditional spirit of humankind.

Though I'm not a god-squadder, I do believe in God. I resonated to the idea of a higher purpose. That was something I could hold onto. The idea a spiritual path actually felt pretty good.

Or maybe I was just grasping at air. When you're desperate, you'll try anything. So, along with weekly therapy and chiropractic care, I tried a variety of "spiritual" approaches. I had my astrology chart read; got readings from a couple of "intuitives"; had several people channel for me; got "integrated energy therapy" from a woman who claimed to talk to angels; listened to various psychics; tried things I'd never even heard of before, like cranial sacral work. (Don't ask.). There was some serious quackery along the way, but there were several credible experiences, too. The good ones, I found, were worth their weight in gold.

None of this, though, could disguise what wasn't there—namely, my wife.

* * *

Off and on through June and July, we connected, disconnected, misconnected, tried to connect again. One Saturday evening, Kelly and I went into town to try out a new Indian restaurant. It was a pleasant enough dinner. No fireworks. That night, Kelly slept alone in the barn, our separation as agonizing as ever. But at least we were trying to find a place of comfort with each other. Sunday was a relaxed day of errands, yard work and watching a movie together. We'd invited two couples over for dinner, which we cooked together in a relatively comfortable atmosphere of small talk. Still no fireworks. The evening proved to be lovely.

As Kelly and I cleaned up afterwards, I noticed that the animation and high spirits she'd shown through dinner were now absent. "Are you okay?" I asked. "You seem sad and somewhat deflated all of a sudden."

"Before I answer that," she responded tersely, "you just make sure the question is about *me* and not about how my feelings make *you* feel or affect *you*."

Boy, was that ever uncalled for. I'd felt only love and concern when I noticed the change in her demeanor. Now, I told her as much. Back and forth we went for the next hour and a half. She'd been triggered by an assumption that I asked the question only to elicit from her what I had done to cause her change of mood. She finally agreed that her response had been controlling, manipulative and based on her experience of our 20 years together. I said, "Thank you," and thought it was over. But it kept on going. She charged angrily that I rambled on and on, and all she could do was listen.

"Bullshit," I said.

She asked what my point was. I responded that I wanted her to accept me for who I am *now*—not pre-judge me based on her view of our past. I reminded her that she'd lectured me a thousand times over the last year not to hang on to the past; that I had to "live in the present." Yet here she was—again—making judgments based on her perceptions of our history together.

This was hardly new terrain for us, but this time there was a subtle shift. Instead of raging or accusing, I made my point calmly. I told her that she had a point about the importance of being in the present—but that *she* had to be there, too.

By now, therapy had helped me begin to face my emotional selfishness and see how my standard response to a threatening situation was to mount a heated defense, throw up walls, protect my turf. I could see how that forced a lot of discussions to focus on me instead of on the other person. I was still a long way from acting on this insight with any consistency, but at least I was facing my destructive pattern, not ignoring or running from it anymore. That Kelly didn't see this growth and still offered responses based on old assumptions frustrated and, yes, angered me. Wasn't she a therapist now? I mean, weren't people in her profession sup-posed to live and practice what they preach? It certainly wasn't happening here. Her 'do-as-I-say, not-as-I-do' attitude wasn't cut-ting it for me any more – as much because I was finally starting to see it.

That night as I lay alone in bed, I realized that I needed to be strong enough to pull out of our old dynamic even if she couldn't. Why was I still taking offense? It was so weak and unhealthy, and it only served to push my wife further away.

"It's not about you," I heard Luke and Janet echo in my head.

All right, so it took a year of therapy and countless conversations with friends. And I was still months from grasping that Kelly's blame game was largely her way of avoiding dealing with her own shit. But at least I was starting to get it now: Kelly's unhappiness wasn't about me. Call it one large step toward reality, one small step toward recovery. Hey, at least it was a start.

9. YOU GOT ME ON MY KNEES

It was not too long ago that Kelly and I would hold hands when we walked together. If we weren't holding hands, she would take my arm while we strolled. Now she strode along parallel to me, hands anywhere but in mine. I felt like I was in the Twilight Zone. It felt foreign not feeling her touch as we walked. It was unnatural. I felt such a void on my right side as we walked now. I didn't know what to do with my arm, my hand, wrist or fingers. My whole right side was orphaned, in mourning.

By now, I understood that the dreaded 'D' word was in play. We were way too far gone not to hear the divorce knell chiming. But I still couldn't help thinking that any minute, Kelly would end this cruel joke with that rousing, "April Fools'!" A day didn't go by that this thought didn't invade my consciousness. As a result, I approached each and every day, each and every encounter, wide open and vulnerable. I'd watch Kelly's gestures, listen to the tone of her voice, gauge the expression on her face, searching for signs of hope. Eagerly, I awaited any crumbs she might drop. When I failed to find them, I was crushed anew. Each time; every time.

To withstand that kind of self-inflicted punishment, I had to find ways to cope. I glommed onto anything that might help ease the pain. *Anything.* Touchy-feely workshops. Psychic and astrology readings. Letters penned to the inner Little Me. Granted, my efforts involved a good bit of flailing. But cumulatively they were chipping away at my self-anaesthetizing paralysis. Slowly, I was beginning to grasp that my life was going to continue, with or without the woman I loved.

Thus, in the spring, feelings began to surface that were not directly connected to Kelly and my marital breakdown. What emerged wasn't pretty. I regarded myself as worthless. Desperate. Lacking in self-esteem or value. De-manned. A "Kick Me" sign was emblazoned on my back, and might have stayed there a whole lot longer were it not for four persistent forces—my lifelines, if you will—that each, in a different way, encouraged me to stop running and start fighting to reclaim my life.

First and foremost, there were my kids. I love them so much. I don't think they ever doubted that. But I needed to reclaim their respect after subjecting them to my weeping, uncontrollable screaming and wasting away, both physically and emotionally. They hadn't signed up for this burden and I was horrified that I hadn't been able to shield them from it. Now, I resolved not to flatten them further with my trauma. I wanted to show them strength. I wanted to put them first again, something I had been unable to do for too many months.

Second, there was my sister, Jill. Practical and wise, Jill listened extraordinarily well and offered sage advice, though she never interfered. It was Jill who made me aware on a daily basis of how much healing was going on. Although I didn't feel it and the pain hadn't subsided, she kept me on track knowing that I was doing the best work I could. She constantly reminded me that healing something this big didn't happen overnight. She couldn't tell it to me enough times.

Third, there was my motorcycle. Or rather Russ's. He had two of them and would lend me one each time we'd go out for long, scenic rides up the Delaware River. This new pastime, my first real hobby ever, was more than a lifeline. It was therapy, a moving meditation, my little corner of heaven. When riding, my worries melted away. For those few minutes or hours, I was calm, happy, at peace with myself and the universe. And it felt like growth to be doing something that, in spite of childhood injunctions, I had decided to do. It felt good to think for myself without the maternal warnings to the contrary always banging away in my subconscious.

Finally, there was Laila, with whom I was now in daily contact. I'm going to digress a moment to tell you a bit about her, since she would play such a pivotal role in my crisis-ridden life. We had met the latter half of my senior year of high school in the Staples Players. She wasn't in the spring production, but she hung around the fringes of the theater group doing tech work. I remember spending a lot of my free time during school hours sitting on the campus lawn talking with Laila. Though she was gorgeous and oozed an ease with her own sexuality, I was probably the only guy at Staples not hitting on her. Happy with my girlfriend Debbie, I just enjoyed talking with her, an approach that threw Laila at first, and then helped her grow to trust me.

Laila was so different from the typical Westport kid. She was from the South and worked hard—though without much success—to rid herself of an ever-present Atlanta drawl. Her background made me want to weep, especially in light of the wonderful and protective cocoon that I had grown up in. Laila's family was a horror story, like something you might encounter in a Tennessee Williams play. Her parents had married straight out of high school and had four kids in rapid succession. Laila, the third (like me, come to think of it), felt invisible. During her early years, she and her family lived in poverty. I remember her telling me how she wore hand-me-down clothes until she was old enough to work and buy her own. She projected sadness as she described how her alcoholic father drank away any chance of a better life. When she was five, her parents divorced. Her two older sisters both had babies at 15. When this tidbit leaked out to the public, Laila's best friend since birth was no longer allowed to play with her due to the shame it brought to the whole family. Parents would call their children inside whenever Laila walked down the street to find her friends to play. Her mother subsequently moved Laila and her younger brother to a run-down section north of the city, but closer to the cultural section – the theaters and museums. Laila was 13 when her mother married a successful actor who'd toured in Atlanta and lived in Westport. Her mother uprooted the remnants of the family and moved with her new husband to Connecticut. Thus began Laila's introduction to one of America's most upscale communities. She felt culturally unprepared and incapable of fitting in. The town's kids, she told me later, were all better than she was because they had "better everything."

In June 1974, my girlfriend Debbie and her family moved to Philadelphia. After 19 months, our relationship had run its course; her move sealed its ending. Throughout that summer, Laila and I did what came naturally. There was no discussion, no coyness, no shyness. We had developed a deep and comfortable friendship. That summer we found ourselves in lust. We had such a good time. We laughed and played, got goofy and didn't give a damn what anyone else thought. She was gloriously uninhibited. I wasn't. Her influence was quick and powerful. She taught me that sex was a "hoot"—at least when I was with her.

Laila was a complicated young woman. She had a desperate need for acceptance and approval which, in part, manifested itself through sexual promiscuity – something girls got *reputations* for, but for which boys doing the same got applauded. Laila was also incredibly intelligent and insightful. Somewhere between the 'sexploits' and constant striving for acceptance was an exceptional intellect. Beyond the hardships life had thrown in her way beat the heart and determination of a lioness. She was real. And in so many ways she was far more grounded than me. It is what made her so damn compelling to me coming out of high school and is what would attract me to her again in mid-life.

Neither of us gave any thought to a serious or permanent arrangement that summer after high school. We just enjoyed our summer of fun and friendship, free of expectation or obligation. When I left for college, there were no tears. That fall, we saw each other several times, usually when I was home on break. Once, she drove down to Princeton to visit. When I came home for spring break, Laila had disappeared. No one had any idea where she'd gone.

We wouldn't cross paths again until the late 1990s, when a high school web site was posted on the internet. Laila's name included an email address, so I popped her a message: "Hey, remember me? Where are you? How are you? What have you done with yourself these 20+ years since you disappeared from the face of the earth without a word or a forwarding address?" Her response, which included a phone number, was short and sweet: "Wow. I never thought I'd hear from *you* again! How are you? I'm fine, remarried and living in the suburbs of Atlanta."

It was like a message from another planet. I called and we had a lovely chat, relaxed, non-threatening, just two old friends getting re-acquainted. She had a daughter from a prior marriage who was ready to graduate high school. She had raised the girl pretty much on her own, was happily married to husband No. 3, and was working an administrative job with a logistics company. I ended the conversation by asking if I could take her to lunch the next time I was in Atlanta. She laughed and said, "Sure. But I guess that means I'll never see you. Nobody in their right mind would ever come here on purpose."

Three weeks later, we had lunch.

Over burgers and fries, Laila told me that leaving Westport had been her first act of bravery and independence. She'd earned one-way airfare back to Atlanta by doing painting and garden work for a local half-way house for teens. When she left, there were no farewell parties, no family to see her off at the airport. She simply packed and left. She commented how comforting and easy it was to slip away unnoticed, calling it a "skill." She continued, "In a low-rent area north of Atlanta, I got an apartment of my own and made do with cast off furniture found discarded along the side of the road. At age 18, I married because I was bored and he was cute. We lived together six months and divorced. No property, no children." Six years later, she married again, this time, she said, to a "pathological liar and borderline schizophrenic." Two years later with a two year old in tow, she got her second divorce. "I swore off men at that point. All they ever caused me was pain any-way," she laughed. "I focused my time and attention on raising my daughter and working three jobs off and on to support the two of us." Eventually, she bought a house, where she now lived with her daughter and her husband of four years, Tom.

As she shared her story, I was mesmerized. She was so grounded. She had shown such courage getting her life in order. To do that with none of the support mechanisms that most of us take for granted, relying on her own resourcefulness, was a marvel to me. Our two hours together flew by and it seemed like we had barely begun to talk.

Over the next two years, we phoned and emailed each other intermittently. Our contact was casual, comfortable, nothing inti-mate. But when Kelly hit me with her disconnect and I tumbled into despair, Laila offered help. One of the first things she did was share what she'd written in her journal the night after our lunch two years earlier: "One hundred and eighty degrees. Complete opposites. Jonathan, the definition of confidence, accomplish-ment and destined success, with every enviable advantage any reasonable person would want, and me with a striking resemblance to the wide-eyed poster child for food stamps, family dysfunction and failure. How could two people whose lives never paralleled in any way—only intersecting briefly—find themselves sharing so much?"

Since then, she'd given generously of her wisdom and insight during our daily phone conversations. She was working at a job that was no more than a paycheck to her. Time she had plenty of. So did I. Still unable to focus on my job, I got by with a minimum amount of work, preferring to talk with Laila, sometimes several times a day. She was now trying hard to rescue marriage No. 3, which she said was being subverted by her husband's lies and deceit. We, of course, discussed the sad state of our respective marriages, offering each other feedback, advice and solace. But there were happier topics, too. Laila was a grandmother now, and loved telling me about her granddaughter. She was also thinking about going back to school to get a college degree. I, in turn, loved describing my motorcycle adventures, and sharing things I'd read in psychology, philosophy, self-help and New Age books, counting on her to help me make sense of it all. Laila was a great sounding board. Schooled in the world of hitting the wall, she was wise beyond her years; though empathetic, she refused to let me feel sorry for myself.

Basically, both of us just needed a safe, nurturing place to unload whatever was on our minds—and we found it in each other. Over the months, we came to lean on each other so heavily that in addition to our chats, we emailed voluminously back and forth. For me, writing satisfied something that talking couldn't. The combination was powerful and wonderful.

Please understand. My love for my wife hadn't waned a bit. But after more than a year of "disconnect," Kelly and I had hit an impasse, and there was no give in either of our positions. She kept talking about wanting us to have a "symbiotic friendship"; I couldn't erase 20 years of marriage and just be her pal. She kept going on and on about my "weaknesses;" I wanted her to accept me, for better or worse, as I was. She spoke constantly of "separation;" I wanted her to find her way back to me. She thought it best if one of us moved out; I longed for my old life, the one where our kids chided, "Get a room." I wanted the closeness and the intimacy back. She was my wife, for god's sake. But I also started to hear the strains of the violin playing at the very corners of my consciousness, whispering, "You never really had such closeness or intimacy with her, Jonathan. It was only the illusion you built over time that you are seeing and feeling." It would take the better part of two more years before I really faced up to that one.

As I neared the one-year anniversary of Kelly's disconnect, I was tiring of facing each day as if it were a battleground to cross beneath a barrage of incoming fire. I was tiring of feeling unloved and unlovable, of waking up alone and lonely in an empty bed. I was tired of the persistent, throbbing, agonizing pain. In the absence of tenderness, intimacy and gestures of affection, I was starting to realize that I would rather face a *fait accomplis* than continue to live in this threatening state of limbo.

I needed a jolt to reawaken me. Laila provided that electric charge.

It's hard to pinpoint the moment my relationship with Laila crossed from platonic friendship into something more intimate. Perhaps it was the day, shortly after my 25th Reunion, that she emailed me digital pictures of her granddaughter. "She's beautiful!!" I responded. "Just like her grandma ..."

"You're so full of bullshit," she emailed back. "But thank you anyway."

Sent: Monday, June 09 3:08 PM

To: Laila

you replied that I'm full of bullshit when I said that you're beautiful. You are. Why would you question it? It's my opinion ... hopefully it's yours too.

Sent: Monday, June 9 4:34 PM

To: Lewis, Jonathan

It's a Southern thing - we may know in our hearts that we are beautiful, but we'll say "Oh no, I'm nowhere near as beautiful as <blank>..." If we simply say "Well, thank you", then we're considered arrogant.

So, in the spirit of your influence, I will say this: Thank you very much for your compliment. I'm really flattered. (God that felt awful!)

I loved the harmless flirtatiousness that was seeping into our communications. Once I logged off or hung up the phone, the hit of adrenalin would evaporate instantly and I'd find myself back in the nightmare that was my life. But for those few minutes (or, so often, hours) each day that I entered this cocoon Laila and I were spinning, I felt appreciated, desirable, even loved. One day, I forwarded Laila one of those emails, sent from friend to friend, that is slightly off color and not business appropriate.

Sent: Friday, June 20 10:14 AM

To: Lewis, Jonathan

Subject: Snip Snip

I LIKE this one. Too bad I can't circulate it around the office. Darn.

Puppy Winston went for his "operation" today. Poor little guy. My squeamish husband acted as though he was losing another member of the Testicle Club. What is it with you guys? They aren't YOURS, you know.

Sent: Friday, June 20 12:15 PM
To: Laila
We men love our testicles. And, since we're such a sympathetic, caring lot, seeing our brethren (of all species) lose theirs, is very emotional and painful. You see, it's our sensitivity ... why can't women understand that? Such an insensitive bunch...!

Sent: Friday, June 20 12:37 PM
To: Lewis, Jonathan
Truth be told - we women love your testicles, too.

A few days later, during a back and forth about her pursuit of photography, she wrote, "Actually, when I set up a modest black & white darkroom in my spare bathroom, I intend to have my daughter take some tasteful nudes of me. Want one?"

Sent: Thursday, June 26 3:55 PM
To: Laila
In triplicate please. And, how about a few 8x10 color glossies?? (Damn, I just broke a sweat ...)

Sent: Thursday, June 26 4:19 PM
To: Lewis, Jonathan
Just a sweat? You can do better than that!
(I think we've "started")

```
Sent: Thursday, June 26  4:24 PM
To: Laila
OK,OK, I confess. It's a 3-legged race from here to
the finish...
    (Yes, I think we've "started" too.)
```

Because we lived 800 miles apart, it was easy to throw ourselves into the sweaty innuendos, yet not take our insinuations too seriously. We both needed a release; our daily phone calls and emails seemed safe places to park our mutually frustrated appetites. Though Laila's marriage was doing a lot better than mine, she was screaming for intimacy. Mostly, we were there to help each other. And that deepened our friendship.

One day, Laila raised the subject of money. She was frustrated and anxious because there was so little of it in her life; she felt powerless to help her daughter and granddaughter. Unable to offer financial assistance because of my changed job status, all I could think to offer was the time-worn chestnut, "Until you have money, you think it's the answer to everything. Only once you have it do you realize that it just presents a whole new set of issues."

```
Sent: Thursday, August 8  10:49 AM
To: Lewis, Jonathan
Subject: Big Lump
I hung up from you with this huge lump in my throat. Not
sure who/what it was for - me, you, our respective kids
who are inevitably hurt by what we do. Money is only
important when you don't have enough to pay for shel-
ter, food, clothes, warmth... beyond that, it means
little to me... I feel empowered to make changes in my
life that contribute to my happiness. Do you?
```

Sent: Thursday, August 8   11:05 AM

To: Laila

Only you can make you happy. (uh oh, sounds like textbook psychobabble to me). You are empowered every day to listen to your inner voice and follow it. It may take you to some strange and unknowing places, but it's always meant to be.

Sent: Thursday, August 8   11:47 AM

To: Lewis, Jonathan

The best times in my life have been when I've listened to my inner voice. My deepest regrets are when I didn't. Thanks for being my friend.

And so it went. Without embarrassment or shame, we leaned on each other, worrying about the other's happiness. A conversation never went by without Laila offering a pep talk. "Any progress today with you and Kelly?" she'd ask. "I know you guys are going to make it, J. It's just a gut feeling of course, but a strong one." She truly believed in Kelly and me, and I clung to her every reassurance. God knows, I needed it. Night after night, I'd look out the bedroom window and, seeing Kelly through a barn window, ache anew. This constant reminder that she was forging a life without me made it hard—sometimes impossible—to sleep.

I don't know what finally prompted me to act. Maybe I was sick of gazing out on a woman who, though only the width of a driveway away, behaved like there was an ocean between us. Maybe I was sick of not sleeping with the woman I loved. Maybe it was her demeaning and condescending tone of voice. Maybe her inability or lack of desire to communicate *any* hope for reconciliation had worn me down. Maybe I was sick of not sleeping, period. Or perhaps it was something else entirely. Maybe Laila and my cyber-panting nudged me across some emotional threshold; maybe I saw what was coming and knew I had to get the hell out of my barren marital bed first. All I know is that one morning in September I woke up understanding that if things continued this way, I would break again.

When my pal Randy, who'd gone through the trenches with his wife before they divorced, offered me a room at his farm house some 20 miles away, I seized the opportunity. From Russ and Mary Ellen I borrowed an air mattress and started spending my nights at Randy's. While I clocked more sleep this way, it did nothing to carve an emotional distance from the life I returned to each morning as I pulled up our driveway. My office was still there. My kids - confused, hurt and angry - were still there. And Kelly, distant and all knowing, was still there.

During this period, the only bright spots in my days were my interactions with my kids and the communications with Laila. In late September, our light-hearted flirtation began to assume a more earnest tone.

```
Sent: Wednesday, October 01   7:56 PM
To: Lewis, Jonathan
Subject: I'm, ah …
    ...I'd say a little tipsy. Okay, then, a lot. I've
been drinking a wonderful new (to me) drink called
Tequiza...Mary Chapin Carpenter is blasting on the
CD, singing "Passionate Kisses"... I realize that Tom
doesn't ever dance with me and that makes me sad. I'm
not a good dancer, and he's even worse, but that's
perfectly fine and irrelevant because there's something
about being gracefully led off your feet and into some-
one's arms just to stand close and move. The ultimate
romantic maneuver for a man to do to a woman - and I
```

mean the ultimate...So, after a few of these Tequiza
things, a young girl's thoughts turn to sex. It isn't
that alcohol makes one hot for the first guy to come
along...I gotta be sorta hot for a guy to start with,
and then the booze is like this glorious Slip N Slide
to pure lust. But back to the sex...

    Do you want to play?

We had just crossed the line. The next morning we talked for a
long time. Were we thinking what we were thinking? I took pains
to make clear what I was feeling. "I've never *ever* cheated on Kelly.
Not even considered it," I told Laila. "In 20 years of marriage, I've
been 100% faithful—not because I had to be, but because I wanted
to be. So why do I want to go against everything I believe? Why do I
feel so comfortable and want this more than anything I've wanted
in a *long* time?"

If I was surprised by my lack of hesitation or absence of guilt,
I had no trouble finding explanations. Fourteen months had now
passed since Kelly and I last made love. (Let me qualify that: she
had consented to have sex with me twice in that period of time,
one of those being on our 20th anniversary. She did it without
desire, without emotion and with the drama of a woman giving in
because it was easier than the alternative. Frankly, it was downright
humiliating.) During that time, my self-esteem and self-worth had
withered. Now here was Laila offering to reawaken and reacquaint
me with these slumbering parts.

As we shared our thoughts about infidelity, we segued into discussing what we wanted to do to each other. Just as in high school,
neither Laila nor I had any inhibitions. Like high school, whatever
inhibitions I had seemed to vanish in her presence, in her ease
and comfort. It was wonderful. When I had to ring off to han-

dle an unavoidable conference call, Laila fired off an email that ratcheted up the heat.

> Sent: Thursday, October 02 2:09 PM
>
> To: Lewis, Jonathan
>
> Subject: For your conference call
>
> I thought it might help with the boredom of those bloodsucking conference calls if I went ahead and told you what I was thinking when we hung up. I'm hoping that you would get worked up, and, at the risk of countering your Wellbutrin, a little distracted from the conversation if I can get you to feel aroused while talking to, say, the CEO. How flattering that would be.
>
> Frankly, your voice is sexy and it arouses me. But I'm sure you've been told that a hundred times. It arouses me in interesting ways…I like it that I can anticipate an email from you outlining what your preferences are and I'm hoping for some detailed imagery such as, me running my tongue up your spine, around your shoulders ending with your mouth brushing mine - no other touching but that.
>
> The lights low and you gently raise my arms over my head and back me up to a wall - always those gentle kisses that we are clearly drawn to but never get - and your hands moving over me, stopping in all the right places (actually, there are only Two Right Places to start with) and lingering long enough so that every part of me becomes the right place to touch. I'll have to show you that place on my shoulder that Tom knows about but neglects most of the time.
>
> I want to hear your voice telling me what to do, how much pressure to apply, how fast to move as I slide down

the wall to my knees and take you in my mouth. I will want to hear when I have it right and am doing what will bring you to climax. I want to know.

More tomorrow. Have a nice conference call.

Sent: Thursday, October 02 2:57 PM
To: Laila

I have GOT to get my heart to slow down ... and the sweat removed from my brow... You definitely accomplished your goal of getting me aroused. So ... here's back at ya':

I want you S L O W. That's the way to start. The lights are low, candles work better. There is gentle music playing/throbbing on the stereo. The room is 2-3 degrees warmer than it should be. I want to feel you sweat - and I want to taste it when it flows.

I need time to kiss you - deeply. You're up against the wall, feet barely touching the ground as I have you pressed up and into it - but gently and with no pain. The bliss comes with the depth of the kiss. Touching begins and it is ever so delicate. Nothing rough, nothing desperate. Erogenous zones can be ignored for now. I'd rather run my fingers along your shoulders and neck - follow it with my tongue. Feel your face, your cheekbones, your hair. Your tongue might find my ear along the way...

Your clothes will come off - but this will take plenty of time... jumping naked right away would only dampen the quality of the arousal. But off they will come - one slow piece at a time. I want to touch every aspect of you. I want to run one finger up and down your chest bone, stopping to appreciate your hips, your navel and belly. A little massage oil only accentuates the sensation. I want to understand the contours of your arms and shoulders. I want to bury my face in your neck, taste the salt on your lower cheekbone and chin. Now I will roll you over ... Explore your spine and shoulder blades. Appreciate your thighs and calves. Rub your feet... Moving ever so slowly...

Sent: Thursday, October 02 8:02 PM
To: Lewis, Jonathan
There isn't enough cold water in the southern hemisphere for me now.

I want this. I want this badly. And, in my mind, I've already spent many hours in the same candle-lit room, warm and relaxed with you, with my head on your chest listening to your heartbeat, allowing myself to ...go into that hypnotic state where every movement is so graceful, purposeless and, yes, so very slow.

I can't remember if we fit well together so many years ago. Maybe I was too silly and clumsy to notice details, but I'll notice them now. I'll notice the way your hips fit between my legs. I'll remember if we get tangled in the sheets and how we maneuver out of them... I'll know how your thighs feel and taste to my tongue. It will stay with me - and oh, God, your voice... when I ask you to TELL me, talk to me, direct me, reassure me, ask me, make no mistake, it's purely selfish. Nothing educational about it - I want to hear you.

Not tomorrow. Tom and I are home all day. But I have some things to think about anyway.

Our unabashed boldness felt natural and right. I wanted more. I found my lack of reserve interesting, but no more than that.

The word "regret" never once entered my mind. Perhaps that's because, as titillated as I felt by Laila's overtures, I never once felt the slightest wavering in my devotion to Kelly. If Kelly (who would accidentally stumble on print-outs of Laila's and my emails months after she'd reached her own conclusions about our marriage) sees that as hypocritical bullshit—well, I can see that. Now. But at the time things heated up between Laila and me, it seemed like apples and oranges. Kelly had left me and tossed in another man to boot. Unprovoked. Moreover, during the agonizing months of our estrangement, another one of her favorite mantras was, "You need to find someone who is as passionate about you as you are about her. Someone who isn't scared of it or your craving for intimacy." After 14 months of tossing alone in bed, contemplating my wife's emotional infidelity, physical infidelity was no longer unthinkable.

> Sent: Friday, October 03 5:52 PM
> To: Laila
> It's the end of another long week and you are once again on my mind. I want you – all of you...

> Sent: Saturday, October 04 7:01 PM
> To: Lewis, Jonathan
> I know what I want to feel and right now; you're making me feel all of it...I want to be the first from these 14 months – really 21 years. My ego wants to be the one who wakes you up and reminds you of everything sensual and aroused that you've left behind to protect yourself. You need to take, too. You need to let me take your head into my hands and let me kiss you slowly, passionately, lightly...
>   *This much I know is true - you make my toes curl.*

Yet even as Laila and I danced closer to the inevitable, I was unable to shake the misery I was feeling at home. The pain-o-meter just kept rising. Many nights as I rolled down the driveway to my exile at Randy's farm house, I would scream uncontrollably. When my emotional floodgates overflowed, screaming was the only outlet I knew for release. I was still a mess. And I poured my pain out daily to Laila.

Sent: Sunday, October 05 11:52 AM
To: Laila

How many ways can I say that I miss my wife so? She is so much a part of me. I love her with a depth that fills every aspect of me. I cannot fathom her disconnect, her distance. I cannot imagine living without her. I cannot imagine our family breaking up. It's not in my frame of reference. I'm a lost soul. She is all that I want. But I know that I am struggling with a ghost of someone I loved and lost...It is so hard for me to accept that she is probably not going to find her way back. I know I have to move on with my life. But I don't want to. It hurts...

Sent: Monday, October 06 10:15 AM
To: Laila

I lost it. I got back to the house for work this morning just as Sarah was getting on the bus. Kelly was so distant, so unreachable. I tried to start a conversation but she just wouldn't go there. She is in as much pain as I am - I only wish that I could penetrate it. She wants no part of me and makes that very clear... Kelly didn't stick around. She feigned something about going to work, jumped in her car without as much as a goodbye, and was gone. I lost it. Laila, I started to

scream. It came from someplace deep and dark and raw.
I just screamed and screamed and screamed. I was flailing. I was jumping up and down, moving aimlessly around
the house and all the while wailing at the top of my
lungs. All that came out was "NO. NO. NO ..." Only when
my voice was completely shot and the dizziness forced
me to sit and put my head between my legs did I stop...
An exorcism perhaps.

Sorry to dump this on you so early in the morning.

Laila, God love her, was willing to feel my pain—but not be a
sucker for my self-pity.

You chose your exorcism through screaming. Not a
bad choice I might add. Short, dramatic - sorta like a
baseball bat to the head. It's over/get better. We'll
work on scream therapy when you come down...

Later that day we agreed to hook up a few days hence in Atlanta.
Actually, I already knew I'd be there for an industry conference,
but this was the moment that Laila and I mutually accepted what
we were up to. After we agreed to spend the coming Friday morning together—in my hotel room—we exchanged lengthy emails
and phone calls. As our seductive dance of words escalated, Laila
began to have reservations.

Sent: Tuesday, October 07 4:23 PM
To: Lewis, Jonathan
Damn. Again, damn. I was panicked this morning, sure
that Tom was going to check my email... Do we know what
we're doing?

Sent: Tuesday, October 07 5:02 PM

To: Laila

I know exactly what we're doing. So do you ... and it's lovely ... I can't think of two finer people who deserve some passion in their lives. And it's entirely without guilt or second thoughts. You're beautiful - in so many ways. I don't want to lose the connection. And guilt will drive a stake right between us. We should talk about it ...

Gently, J

Sent: Tuesday, October 07 6:51 PM

To: Lewis, Jonathan

We do need to talk about guilt, because I'm having a great deal of it.

But about talking - don't you sense the danger in the emotional connection as well as the intense physical longing? You think distance is going to ensure someone doesn't get hurt? There's an emotional payoff going on here, too. Otherwise neither of us would listen to the other for as long as we do, or be as tolerant of the time we're taking. Is it about sex? Absolutely. Is it playful? No doubt - wonderfully so. Passion? Passion such as I haven't felt in a very, very long time and I may be willing to risk a lot for it.

Soft kisses, L

Sent: Tuesday, October 07 8:24 PM

To: Laila

As for guilt, I think this last 14 months has inured me to it. Based on the joy I get in talking with you, emailing back and forth, and ultimately the short

I THOUGHT WE WERE HAPPY

times we will have together, there is absolutely no
guilt. None. Nada. Zippo. And I don't want to lose this
- it's too special. That said, I don't want to be the
reason for your divorce, if you and Tom come to that. If
I'm a catalyst to help you face issues, great. But I
can't be the reason. And I'm sure you agree in return.

Tenderly, J

Sent: Wednesday, October 08 4:16 PM

To: Lewis, Jonathan

If leaving Tom were my agenda, I had the perfect
opportunity day before yesterday. He suggested it and I
didn't argue. It wasn't until the next morning that I
realized losing him is not something I want to allow. We
have too much on our side to throw in the towel. But I
would be lying if I said I didn't have feelings for you
that go beyond sex and lust. As we've said more than
once, I can leave the sex behind on a moment's notice,
but the relationship we've developed as friends means a
lot to me...I intend to hold you to your promise that
we won't lose that. Do you understand how important
that is? It has *nothing* to do with staying with or
leaving Tom.

Me

Sent: Wednesday, October 08 5:13 PM

To: Laila

The friendship will never be lost. That you can count
on. And I have to believe you and I will go through many
iterations of our relationship over the next 25 years
as our immediate personal lives go through their twists
and turns. The physical side of you and me is something

160

we both want to explore much more completely... I look forward to Friday so much I want to burst.

Lovingly, J

Sent: Thursday, October 09 9:38 AM

To: Lewis, Jonathan

...For you, I represent exploration - the opening of some box you put yourself in years ago. Off flies the lid and I feel like you're reaching out, flailing and railing against a safe, self imposed sensory deprivation. I have a sense that the arm helping you to steady is my sexuality, honesty, lack of inhibition. I definitely serve a purpose here. I'm up to it.

But me...I'm not able to right myself as easily. As I said and believe me I meant it - I'm fiercely monogamous...I thought when I started the emails that I was starting simple foreplay, but I've ended up tapping into some profoundly compelling needs... I will never be able to be honest with Tom again after I meet with you alone on Friday. There's the rub...

Will you come to Atlanta because I need you or I miss you, or will it be just when business pays the tab? That's too cavalier an arrangement for me to risk what I value most...

Tonight's bottom line. I don't care. I just want to be with you, and I now know that's going to happen. And after all this crazy prattle, do you still want me?

Eager for Tomorrow Morning, L

Looking back, I see this as the point where she exposed her vulnerability. We both had a need for each other. Her ability to articulate something so much more than raw physical desire was evident — but I'm not sure that I was paying it the attention it deserved. In fact, I was way too self-absorbed and focused on my own pain to even consider it. Looking back, that's a huge regret. She was such a good friend and deserved more from me than I gave her. I fired off another email.

> Yes, I still want you... My sanity is at stake, not to mention aspects of self-respect and my own manhood... Is this just a passing, fleeting fancy? No, I don't think so. Yes, right now it is business that brings me to Atlanta. You have Tom, I have Kelly. To this point, it shouldn't have been anything else. But, the rules have changed because our partners have changed. So we in turn now change. If you need me or want me, I'm there - with or without the business expense. It's not about convenience; it goes way past that...
>
> I still want you. Plain & simple...
>
> Intimately, J

Our morning together happened as naturally as two good friends getting together for drinks after work. There was no tension, no nervousness, no uneasiness. We met in the hotel's restaurant for breakfast, but stayed only long enough to make a show at drinking a cup of coffee. Then we spent four amazing hours together in Room 1117. It was a beautiful blend of passion, intimacy and rawness. Four hours wasn't enough time. And its aftermath elicited no guilt or second thoughts—for me, that is.

> Sent: Saturday, October 11 8:57 AM
>
> To: Lewis, Jonathan
>
> J,I can't remember a time when I've been so conflicted between knowing what I should do and knowing what I

want. Yesterday morning I wanted only you. You (we)
have disrupted my life, my marriage, my very values,
and I'm wondering if you know what you're doing to me...

I don't know if I can allow us to be together this
way again, I don't know if I can't. We need so much
more time to explore each other...Can't I/we have that
just once more before our circumstances require an end,
before you give this to someone else?...Are you aware
of what you do to me?

-unyielding, softly- L

Maybe I didn't allow myself to acknowledge quite yet that I was disrupting her life. Or maybe I did and chose to ignore it. I was still hiding inside my protective cocoon. I hadn't yet learned to confront my feelings as openly and honestly as Laila did. I had a lifetime of *not* facing what was right in front of me. I can't believe that I didn't understand what she was saying about where our relationship was taking her emotionally. Yet I chose not to address it—at least not yet.

Instead, I made it about me. Just what Kelly said I had done to her for 20 years.

Laila, I don't want to disrupt your life.

So many of your described emotions are similar to what
I experienced Friday morning. Thank you for reminding
me that I am a strong, emotional, vulnerable, attrac-
tive and passionate human being. Kelly has methodi-
cally taken so much of that away from me, but that is
my choice to interpret it as such. No one can actually
do those things to you, only one's self can allow it in
to fester and rip my insides to shreds. I could have
chosen to just hold my head up and walk away...

        I am only now realizing that I'm not an aggres-
    sive lover; I need gentleness, slow movement, time to
    savor and a blurring of the lines when we don't know if
    it's you in control or me. God, when did you roll on
    top of me and take over - I don't remember; when did
    your fingers stop touching me and your tongue start? I
    couldn't sense the transition. THAT's what I want with
    you. It is so satisfying, intimate and fulfilling. My
    body is in its own state of recovery. I seemed to have
    no stamina (oh, such a surprise after 15 months of no
    use and deep depression) but that didn't last long,
    did it? It actually is awakening me to a whole new
    world of possibilities. And you and I need to explore
    them. Again. Soon...

For the briefest moment, I felt whole again. I felt human. I felt
like a man. Quickly, I figured out a way to get back down to Atlanta
later that month, but Laila had doubts.

        Sent: Tuesday, October 14 11:47 AM
        To: Lewis, Jonathan
        I'm feeling a need to back off from all of this. It's
    too "splintering"...This is wrong. I'm your friend. I'm
    cheerleading captain for you and Kelly repairing what's
    broken in your marriage and you getting your life back
    - new and improved. That's all I can/should be. I'm
    sorry, but please let's let the 28th just pass without
    me, okay?

I understood and told her so. Despite my carnal desire to see
her again, I did not want to hurt her. I cherished her friendship;
I didn't want to sacrifice that for a few hours of physical pleasure.

Despite her turmoil, Laila put her own emotions on the back burner to address my neediness. Looking back, I realize how difficult it must have been for her to set her fears and panic aside. I am awed by how, despite her own confusion, she was able to see my situation with such clarity. Laila was real. She didn't play in the daily dramas I was so used to. She was grounded and clear about what she thought, what she wanted and what she feared. Laila was my gift from god. Her email continued.

> You flipped like a switch. There was that point at which you curled up around a pillow, almost in a fetal position and started talking...Bear with me here, and don't be offended, okay? I offer this stuff to help, and only as questions. You must know by now that I'm crazy about you (if you don't, you're a dunderhead)...
>
> You've said more than once you are "A Lewis", and that Lewiss do, or don't do, this or that. You almost use the royal "We". You were born with advantages, maintained those advantages, benefited from them and learned to rely on them at every turn...I asked you if you'd ever really been kicked in the stomach by life and your reaction seemed to indicate you hadn't. When you were growing up did you please people around you by always doing what was expected? The relentlessly confident, happy jock - always smiling?
>
> Fast forward and Jonathan's life has been pretty easy. You married a wonderful woman, built a wonderful, impressive career, your resume reads like Who's Who, you have three wonderful children - you're a great father, a great provider and you live in an upscale neighborhood in what I assume must be a really gorgeous house. You've done exactly *what a Lewis is supposed to*

do ...For you it was identity, but for Kelly was it just a veneer? Not suggesting, just asking. You made people happy when you were strong, in control and confident. Kelly may have gotten lost in your tireless confidence and success. She may feel too far behind (or ahead?!) to close the distance.

You kept saying "I know I'm supposed to be learning something but I don't know what that is." You seemed more frantic about the not knowing part than about the actual lesson. That seemed a control issue to me. Loss = out of control. Okay for me, maybe, but not for you?

Not knowing is okay. Incredible. She had just struck at the heart of my confusion and what it would take to overcome it. I was spending a tremendous amount of money on my therapist – maybe I should have just listened to Laila instead. She continued:

You truly have suffered tremendous losses in the past year and you have every reason to be depressed, angry, scared, off-center. You would be a sociopath if you didn't feel the way you feel. I know as well as anyone how real your suffering is. There's a big difference between you and me. I know that I can, on a Friday afternoon, lose my house, my job, have the transmission fall out of my car, have my electricity turned off, and by the next Friday I'll have a new home, a new job, a new car - - but only because I've experienced those things, dug myself out of miserable holes only to survive stronger and smarter for the next one I manage to tumble into or dig for myself...

But just look how far you've come! You have a very different voice now than you did. You've changed a

lot. You used to equate weakness with failure, and
you almost refused to accept any other alternative for
yourself, because maybe to do so would mean it would
sneak up and destroy you. Now I see you searching for
depth and meaning and the emotional resourcefulness to
not just survive, but flourish with added dimension to
your spirituality and sense of joyful purpose...

Maybe that's the lesson. Accept the fact that your
entire life is not pre-ordained and toss yourself into
unknown, uncontrollable adventure. With or without Kelly,
you'll have to re-evaluate what you want out of life...

You are an extremely compelling man. You have no
idea. You aren't just "bright", "interesting" and "per-
suasive" ... You have off-the-charts benevolent intui-
tion about people that's rarely wrong...And you have
the most sensuous kiss I've ever experienced. I could
go on. Want me to? I will.

You just don't know how to live by the seat of your
pants, sweetheart ... But you will ... You don't have
much choice.

Lovingly, L

She was amazing. And I, as she so aptly put it, was a dunder-
head. Still a good nine months from even beginning to truly appreciate and benefit from the depth of Laila's wisdom and insight, I
instead focused on the possibility of another rendezvous. Over the
next two weeks, our magnetic attraction trumped her doubts. On
October 28th, we spent another morning in another anonymous
hotel room on the outskirts of Atlanta. That night, I emailed her:

It's after 10:00 and I'm tired. But I feel so quiet
and calm and very content. What a beautiful morning it

was. I can't think of a nicer way to have spent it. Why does a simple 'thank you' sound so hollow??

But thank you. Thank you for your passion. Thank you for your friendship. Thank you for talking to me with a clarity that is staggering. Your insights are laser focused and so on the money. And thank you for your crazy wonderfulness and reckless abandon. It teaches me so much about myself and what I need to be and this control thing I need to let go of.

You are such a gift.

Sent: Wednesday, October 29 6:41 PM

To: Lewis, Jonathan

I understand what you mean when you say thank you. It isn't hollow. I'm fairly certain I know what I mean to you, where I fit, and I'll be so comfortable there... You need to know I would give a lot to be with you again, and you also know why that can't happen. But the thought of your touch will always make me close my eyes and catch my breath and go over you in detail... I was paying very close attention.

What you gave me in those short four hours was remarkable and indescribable...It can't possibly be over. Changed I'll accept, but not over... I thought we were extraordinarily beautiful together.

So did I. But her generous attentions didn't dull the incredible want I continued to feel. I ached for the love of my wife. I wanted the passion I felt for and received from Laila coming instead from Kelly. I yearned, keenly, painfully, for my family. Just the thought of the five of us around the dinner table, enjoying a meal together, could make me well up. Still camped out at Randy's, I missed the comfort of my kids hanging around the house with their friends while Kelly and I curled up on the couch watching a movie. Weekends were particularly difficult. Randy's farm house was 20 miles from nowhere, and I didn't feel like I could drop in on my home; the pain of knowing I couldn't reach out to Kelly was still way too big for that. So, except for Mike's hockey games, I was pretty much alone. And lonely. And hating every minute of it.

And why wouldn't I? Incredible as it may seem, up to this point in my life, I'd never lived by myself. In a sense, I'd sculpted my life around *not* living alone. I'd gone from my parents' home (seven in residence) to a series of college suites (usually four in residence) to a house that I co-owned with my brother (five in residence) to a series of homes that I'd bought with Kelly (ultimately five in residence, plus assorted dogs and cats). My new solitude made me anxious, scared, restless and, yes, angry.

> Sent: Saturday, November 15   11:08 PM
> To: Laila
> [My son's hockey team] won tonight, 8-1. The other team was outright dirty, so a lot of testosterone got slung around the ice. Lots of fun to watch. Some thug from the other team jumped Mike late in the game. Mike's usually pretty passive and skates away from the stupidity. But this kid got in his face and started to get physical. Mike pummeled him, I mean, really pummeled him. The ref saw the whole thing, threw the hooligan out of the game and only gave Mike a five minute misconduct penalty. I should be ashamed – I found myself screaming for him to beat the ever-loving piss out of the kid and was cheering him on as he got the better

of the altercation. All I could think was, "That's my boy!" Maybe I need more therapy. I'm so ashamed. Not...

Sweet Dreams, Sweet Woman. J

Mike's games were my highlights of each week. It was our time together. But I was beginning to learn the horror of holidays from the perspective of a broken family.

Sent: Thursday, November 27 10:21 PM

To: Laila

Thanksgiving has never been as depressing as it was today. It's tough to be upbeat and happy when things are so strained. Given the circumstance though, we pulled it together and made the best of it. We all helped cook the holiday meal with all the appropriate trimmings. It was nice playing in the kitchen with the kids. But this was the first Thanksgiving in our entire 20 year marriage that it wasn't celebrated with extended family (usually mine). Sad.

I slept very well (which is unusual) but I also slept very alone last night...That's not going to change for a while and it crushes me every night. Am I just living in a fantasy world that she'll find her way back into our marriage?

C and I are talking a lot. She's a total mess and quickly plummeting toward rock bottom. She has no capacity to give anything to me right now (not that she has over the past year) - which is actually good. In this place, finally she's not blaming me nearly as often about my anger at her rejection, how hard she's tried for 20 years, how wronged she's been, etc. Rather, she appears to be looking deep inside herself at who she

is. And she's coming up blank. It doesn't even begin
to put our marriage back together. But it's a start.
It's just that it hurts so much and I want her back so
badly. Sigh...

Kelly's father passed away a couple of days later. Between the
funeral and the holidays, Laila and I didn't have much contact
over the next few weeks. When we did, our communications continued to sizzle with desire. But all I wanted, thought about and
prayed for was Kelly's love. I was still begging God for my wife's
return. I even negotiated "deals" with Him. You gotta' *know* how
desperate I was when I promised the Big Guy that I would go to
synagogue every Sabbath if He could just see his way to leading
Kelly back to me.

Laila was no less determined to rescue her marriage. Over a
long phone call, she told me assorted stories of her marital ups and
downs with Tom. She said she loved him very much; she just wanted
him to be more intimate and passionate about her. Sort of like us.

Over the next week, we talked a lot about what we meant to
each other. We agreed that our marriages were way too important to abandon—but, hey, wouldn't it be interesting if we were
both spouse-less and living in closer proximity to each other? The
hypothetical got us both so juiced that we made plans for a third
assignation, this one for the last Wednesday in January.

Then reality came crashing down.

Sent: Monday, January 26 7:08 PM
To: Lewis, Jonathan
    Extreme anxiety is coming over me - guilt, fear.
I think Tom knows or at least suspects. I'm horribly

uncomfortable. Duplicity is hard for me. I hate this betrayal.

But I want you, and I want him. While I know I'll have you with or without the physical aspects of our relationship, I *want* your "aspects" very, very much. I know you'll say that there's something about us that transcends the ugliness of infidelity-something about our relationship that makes it elegant...I agree when I'm feeling lusty a safe 1000 miles away from you, but I twist on a rusty, emotional, guilt hook 36 hours prior to your arrival – for more reasons than you know.

I'm too much trouble, Jonathan. I'm too emotional. Dump me.

Now.

But Wednesday morning I'm counting on touching you gently; resting my head on your shoulder and hearing you laugh. I'm simply counting on you...

panicking (again) L

Sent: Monday, January 26   8:17 PM
To: Laila

Thank you again for the trust – and risk – you are taking with me... Please don't turn back. The risks are SO worthwhile because what will come out the other end is so magnificent. Not knowing how it will turn out is the hardest part...Have faith. Have trust. Don't look back and don't try and figure out what tomorrow brings – just stay in it today...

Oh, Laila. Here I sit and lecture you on the philosophy of life and living in the present – and it is the one thing I still cannot do...I am trying so hard to just let go. It is such an oxymoron (letting go shouldn't be a struggle) — I just have to give in to it and let it happen...

So Tenderly, Jonathan

That Wednesday when we met again in another anonymous hotel room, it was everything we wanted it to be—and then some. If there had been any lingering doubt about our feelings for each other, it was dispelled that morning. But where were we going to go from here? Over the next few weeks, that question dominated our phone conversations and emails.

Sent: Wednesday, February 11 5:02 PM

To: Lewis, Jonathan

...what I really want is to go somewhere with you — anyplace as long as it's very far away — and not come back for a long time. I feel a deep sense of needing to be rescued, although I can't quite put my finger on from what. I'm fighting running away again — from some indefinable fear that I'm never going to trust anything I feel ever again and that I'm going to die with this f-cking noose of my past around my neck.

The irony is Tom has been kinder to me than ever. He's more affectionate and considerate. He hasn't been trying to hurt me or be cruel, although I felt the same sort of panic as if he had been. Look at what I've done. Look at what I've been thinking and feeling. I'm the only one who can put a stop to all this.

I feel like I'm just falling and I see everything I value as being really nothing at all — nothing I can depend on, nothing solid and tangible and safe to hold on to, but everything unrevealing, covert, fearful and downright vaporous. I DON'T *KNOW.* And today, I have a rather pathological need to *know,* although I can't quite identify exactly what it is I need to find out.

Sent: Wednesday, February 11 7:24 PM
To: Laila
Please don't run. At least not away from me... Faithful to a fault, I will *always* be there for you. It won't make a difference whether we continue romantically or not. The friendship is what is sacrosanct. It's what I love most about you. Your honesty, openness and vulnerability...

I understand your dilemma. I, too, would love to run away with you for a long, long time. For me it wouldn't be to be rescued but rather for the emotional intimacy, gentleness and healing affect you have on me. I so much want to curl into you and breathe in your scent, your emotions, your earthly sensibilities. You ground me at a time when my feet are planted anywhere but solidly on the ground. It's probably not in the near-term cards as we are both trying to sort out our crazy, off-balance lives. But never say never...

Our romance ended abruptly on February 14, Valentine's Day.

Sent: Saturday, February 14 9:05 AM
To: Lewis, Jonathan
Subject: You'd better sit down
It's not good.

Tom pretty much knows everything. How, I'm not sure. Part of what he knows, he thinks he knows, but he's far too close to the truth and it scares me. He's going over the phone bills, checking dates, "connecting dots," he

says, and he "knows" about our day together. I did not
correct him.

I'm drowning in paranoia now - wondering what he'll
figure out next. The phones aren't secure, email isn't
secure...This has been wrong from the beginning, so
I'm calling it. If Tom and I make it through this mess
I've created, he and I have created, then it will be a
miracle. Our marriage has been damaged whether I want
to admit that or not. And maybe for you this is just
friendship, but I've known for a long time it's more
than that for me, and maturity should have dictated
that I shut this down the minute that became clear to
me. I do know better.

I'm sorry. I love you, Jonathan.

Laila

I respected her wishes and backed away gracefully. Following
her lead, I let our communications dwindle to a sporadic trickle.
How could I not? I wanted for Laila what I wanted for myself: a
resuscitated marriage. And I owed—still owe—Laila boundless
gratitude. She reawakened far more than my numbed senses; she
jogged my very sense of self.

One email, one phone conversation, and yes, one tryst at a
time, she played an enormous role in bringing me back to life.
By rekindling my sense of worth, by reawakening my passion, by
accepting my gentler attentions, she made me realize that my life
was not coming to an end. With or without Kelly—a prospect I still
couldn't wrap my mind around—there was much to live for.

But holding onto that perspective was particularly difficult at
this juncture. For at almost the same moment that Laila decided
she no longer had room in her life for me, so did Kelly.

10. SNAP!

In early December, Kelly got the call from her older sister in Florida, where my in-laws spend their winters. Their 84-year-old father was fading rapidly. Alzheimer's and the ravages of old age had finally caught up with him. The doctor was giving Walter a few days, maybe only hours. Kelly was a mess. Hastily, I made her flight arrangements, and the next morning drove her to the airport. Then, I went straight to Randy's house, picked up my few belongings and, after three months of camping out, moved back into the house—my house. I wouldn't leave again.

A day later, my father-in-law passed away at home, with his wife and three daughters by his side. It was an occasion to both mourn and rejoice. Walter had lived a long, productive life. But the last few years had not been kind. That he went quietly and without pain was a blessing.

Lea called and asked me to deliver the eulogy at his memorial service. Touched and honored, I flew to Florida a few days later. During the three nights we shared a couch bed, Kelly was able to let me hold her only one night while she cried for her father. Otherwise, I kept my hands to myself, knowing that she would regard any physical contact as insensitive to her needs. She had made that so vividly clear over the previous months. Her father's death didn't change that demeanor. My restraint made me ache. I longed to comfort her, to reach out and hold her. To look deep into her eyes and make her see the love and compassion I felt for her. As we lay side by side, I entertained visions of her returning to our home, our marriage, our bed.

Nice fantasy. Kelly flew home with me after the Memorial Service, but didn't stay long. A week before Christmas, she returned to Florida with Sarah for the long holiday. I, in turn, took Mike and three of his buddies to Vermont to ski. Alex chose to remain behind at a friend's house. For five days, we stayed at my in-laws' summer place and did most of our skiing at Killington. God love teenagers; these high school seniors knew how to have fun. I found myself smiling and laughing at their antics. For the first time in a very long time, I relaxed. While they snowboarded, I skied. It was a shot of adrenalin being in their youthful energy field.

To save money, I cooked meals at the house. But the last night, I offered to take them out to dinner. Their unanimous choice was sushi. We piled into the car and descended upon an upscale Japanese restaurant on the access road to Killington. The boys were in a boisterous mood and didn't mellow as we entered the place. Heads turned. Quickly, the hostess put us into one of those private rooms with a sliding door, where you sit barefoot and cross-legged on the floor. If this quarantine was intended to flag the proprietors' disapproval, the boys missed the signal. They were ecstatic. Cool room, dude!

Apparently all the boys had seen some movie in which a character snorts wasabi (that hot, green mustard junk) through a straw. After the sushi arrived, it didn't take long for the testosterone-driven dares to begin. I never laughed so hard in my life. Collin met the challenge first, bravely laughing as his eyes teared with pain. With their manhood at stake, the other three couldn't back down. One by one, they followed suit. Me, I just sat back and laughed. I figured I'd already taken it in the nose more than enough from Kelly.

The only tears I shed that night were the kind that come from laughing too hard.

Kelly returned home in worse shape than when she left. Visibly crumbling, she was so wrapped up inside herself that for that short respite, she didn't blame me for everything wrong in her life. Whole days would go by where I wasn't chastised or reprimanded for anything, be it emptying the dishwasher too loudly, washing the dishes too exuberantly and thus splashing a little water on the counter, or vacuuming the floors too quickly. In early January, she told me that she was going to move some furniture over to Russ and Mary Ellen's newest place. "I need a place to go to rest and have peace," she said.

Russ and Mary Ellen had recently purchased the house, with the intention of converting it into an office for their consulting business. Perfect though it was, there was a hitch: the township had just rejected the parking variance they needed to make the facility viable. The place was now back on the market. In the meantime, Kelly was welcome to use it, free of a rent we couldn't afford.

Initially, Kelly's absence didn't ignite my fears. This didn't feel like a total separation; it was just a prudent distancing so that Kelly could decompress for several hours each day. But as the weeks passed, our communication grew no stronger, and our mutual anger and resentment grew no weaker. At the end of the month, she moved out altogether.

I thought I was going to die. This wasn't like the breather I'd taken at Randy's, where I knew I'd return home each morning to my office, my children—my wife. This was a real separation, the one Kelly had been pressing for almost 18 months, one over which I had no control. It triggered a new wave of panic. Janet, who supported the move, repeatedly reminded me that she'd suggested a separation long ago as the only way to repair our marriage. That bit of I-told-you-so didn't reassure me one bit.

No matter how hard I tried or how many therapy sessions I sat through, I couldn't stop loving Kelly and yearning for her emotional return. Now I added her physical return to the wish list. She would have none of it, nor was she kind or gentle about it.

I told her often how deeply I missed her, how much I loved her. I couldn't say enough times that the mere prospect of seeing her face or hearing her voice still gave me a thrill, an adrenaline rush reminiscent of new romance. To Kelly, I was just being weak. Her response was as consistent as it was terse.

"Well what am I supposed to do with that?" she'd snap back at me.

She wanted out and I still wasn't willing to accept it.

My imagination ran wild. I could only see our separation as an opportunity for Kelly to feel free to see other men—a prospect with which I could never *ever* come to grips. The electrician thing was bad enough. Now, I obsessed about further dalliances. It ate away at me like battery acid. Though Janet, Russ and Mary Ellen kept telling me that the only relationship Kelly was working on was the one with herself, I couldn't see it. If only I had understood...

Instead of easing our tensions, living apart only made it worse— for me. My panic that Kelly would never come back refused to abate. The fear that she might be dating someone made me see red. I got angrier and angrier as my insecurities simply grew wilder, which only pushed her further away. I was an idiot.

You're probably thinking, "*You* had your dalliance with Laila; why couldn't you handle the idea of Kelly having a fling?" Fair question, one for which I have no good answer— *except* this: I was so in love with my wife; she wasn't in love with me. My affair never would have happened, never even would have occurred to me, had I entertained any hope that Kelly would find her way back to me. But her rejection was complete. She gave me no hope. She had not a warm word for me. I needed to recapture my life, my self-esteem, my manhood. Let me say that differently: they had been pulverized during the previous 14 months. I jumped into bed with Laila to jump-start my zombified brain cells.

I know. That explains nothing. But it's the best I can do. I'm not blaming Kelly. *She* didn't make me do it; *I* made me do it. After so many months of rejection, I needed some sort of affirmation, and it sure as hell wasn't coming from the person I most wanted it to come from. Is that a double standard? Does that make me a chauvinist prick? I don't know. I just know that I had to do something to feel human again. Kelly could not, and would not, articulate *anything* that even vaguely suggested she gave a damn about me. She gave me no hope.

By now, what I thought of as "our marriage" no longer existed for her. Instead, she referred to our union as "the marriage,"–as if our 20 years as husband and wife not only didn't exist, but had never existed at all. I found her formulation beyond hurtful; it was despicable.

While Kelly and I lived apart, the boys chose to stay at the house with me. Not wanting to face what might lie ahead, they buried themselves in their friends and girlfriends. Sarah spent the days and most weekends with me, but slept most nights at her mom's. Thankfully, she seemed comfortable floating between both places.

It was because of my kids that I was able to maintain a modicum of good sense—at least when it came to my children. Saddened by the turmoil Kelly and I had imposed on them, I worked hard to support their needs and not get in their way. With the renovation now complete, our house was once again Grand Central Station for all three kids and their large circles of friends. On any given Saturday or Sunday morning, as many as two dozen sleeping youths could be found strewn across carpets, couches and beds. Parents no longer bothered to call to make sure it was okay for their sons and daughters to sleep over, or to check if it was "safe" for their children. They knew I loved these kids and our house was a haven out of harm's way. But they probably didn't know what peace and joy I took from all this wonderful energy. These kids restored my faith in humanity. Far from giving me grief, Mike's friends were actually quite protective of me. To a man, none entered or left the house without offering me a hug. Now that they are off at college, I miss them terribly.

Kelly and my experiment in living apart was a disaster for our relationship—or what remained of it. I couldn't deal with the reality of her absence. Instead, I masked my fear of a permanent split with anger. At every opportunity, I got in her face. "How could you abandon your family like this?" I demanded over and over. No matter what she said or how she said it, I responded with blame, judgment, anger, guilt trips. You can imagine how productive *that* was.

She was in her "I need separation" mind set; I was supposed to be all right with that. No, I was supposed to be better than all right with that. To hear her tell it, I was supposed to love her so much that the emotional devastation she had wrought over these two years was understandable, forgivable, perfectly all right. I was supposed to believe that she didn't want the divorce—that she was only asking for the divorce out of respect for me. I was supposed to find hope in all that she *didn't* say.

"I keep thinking that maybe this whole thing is about me learning how to love and you learning how to accept," she mused more than once.

"Accept what, Kelly?"

"I keep wondering, do you really want to get to know who I really am? Should I even invest or present myself to you? You're so angry. I've never had a strong sense of myself; I've always been such a façade. I don't want to be vulnerable and not matter. I don't know how to uncover the parts of me that are real. Is your anger so big that who I am doesn't matter?"

Her blame would only trigger my sarcasm. "Angry? How could I possibly be angry?" I'd respond. "You betray me, reject me, tell me you love another man and may *never* have been in love with me, and you wonder why I might be angry? You fire salvo after salvo of dime store therapy at me like 'this is about journey and discovery' yet cannot and will not look me in the eyes and say you give a damn about me or our marriage. And then you tell me to 'focus on what I have, not what I don't'? Let me tell you what I have, Kelly. I have *nothing*."

"You should be the person who helps me, Jonathan," she'd reply, adroitly sidestepping my issues to return to hers. "I don't know how to do this. I'm asking for your help. You've been with me for a very long time. I am so vacant and empty and have been my whole life. I want you to know me. I want you to see why I am the way I am, why I'm so scared of you and why I'm so screwed up. I don't know how to be in this world, I don't know the rules. I've lost everything, don't you get that?"

"What you lost is what *you* gave up," I'd fire back. "You betrayed and rejected me in such a horrible fashion. You asked *me* for divorce, not the other way around. How am I supposed to feel gentle, protective and loving to a woman who, after 21 years of marriage, cannot ... no... *will* not show or articulate *any* love or caring? You can't even tell me that you give a damn. Where is the compromise in that? Why must it only be your way or no way?"

"Can't you say that without blame?" she'd demand. "Can't you present it in another, more respectful way?"

"Respectful, Kelly? What respect have you shown me these ugly 18 months?"

And round and round we'd go. It was painful for me – and more than a little confusing. Here was this woman who went back to school in mid-life to get an advanced degree in counseling. She was a junior shrink for god's sake. I had been so excited that she had found a vocation that she loved, that brought out her passion. I had so vociferously supported it. Yet here she was acting so damn inappropriately – or at least that's the way it seemed to me. She was getting away with something, but I couldn't quite get my mind around what it was. Whatever it was, it was most certainly chock full of self-righteousness.

In early March, I invited Kelly to breakfast. We met at one of our favorite local eateries and the best I can say is that we had a non-confrontational meal together. Afterward, we sat in her car and continued to talk. It got a little contentious, over what I don't remember. What I do remember—vividly—is her tag line: "I think it's time we get divorced."

I'm not sure if I was hurt or relieved. Certainly I wasn't surprised. Since her dad's funeral, Kelly had been a mess. If she was clear about anything, it was that she didn't want to see me, spend time with me, talk to me about anything but the kids. She certainly wasn't doing anything to work on our marriage. For me, her virtually complete severance of communication was tantamount to divorce anyway. So, instead of falling apart or going ballistic on her, I looked at her for a long sad moment, then quietly said that I understood. If this was what she wanted, then okay.

Later in the day, she caught me off guard when she phoned the house to ask if I was game to see a new marital therapist with her. A guy named Kilian, complete with Ph.D in couples psychotherapy, came highly recommended by a partner in Kelly's counseling practice who had used him through her own divorce. According to Kelly's colleague, Kilian was savvy at cutting through the bullshit and getting to the core issues. In this colleague's case, the "reality" had turned out to be that she and her first husband were totally unsuited for each other. Gee, *that* sounded promising.

Two days later, I went to see Janet for what turned out to be my last session with her. I told her I was writing a book, and that Kelly had asked for a divorce. Janet's responses were interesting.

*Writing was a good outlet for my feelings; it would open me up. That turned out to be an understatement!

*By asking for the divorce, Kelly had to make a decision and close the door on our marriage; she couldn't drag this separation out any longer.

* Now that she'd requested a divorce, Kelly could no longer blame me for her problems and use me for her whipping boy.

*Since there was no indication Kelly would ever come back to me, I was romanticizing my relationship with her. That illusion would disintegrate when I felt real love returned.

*Stop trying to make Kelly love me; all I do is dissolve each time she rejects me.

As I headed down her office steps for the last time, Janet's final words echoed in my head: "Jonathan, remember that there is the strong possibility that your feelings for Kelly are a fantasy and an illusion. When you change your perception of the situation, you will then be able to get on with your life."

Ouch.

The following day, Kelly and I had our first session with Kilian. If I ever thought before that nothing would be the same, now I knew it for sure. This guy was tough, but incredible; he earned my trust and respect almost immediately. Within minutes of sitting down, he told Kelly it was obvious that she couldn't feel love from anybody. After a lifetime of feeling tolerated at best, how could she possibly feel anything but inadequate? She'd grown up under the iron fist of a controlling father with a narrow view of the world that he imposed on her. How could she not but feel inadequate? As for me, Kilian took stock of my defensive nature and concluded what

Kelly had been saying all along: "You *do* make it all about you." After that one-two punch, he delivered a strong message. "There is no blame for either of you. It's how you constructed your lives and your marriage. You built those parameters from the start. So our starting point is this: *the failure of your marriage is nobody's fault.*"

At the end of the second hour, he summed up what he'd observed. "Being in trouble sits over your marriage and always has. My guess is that it goes back to your respective childhoods where you played the roles of dutiful son and daughter. Kelly just wanted to be acceptable; Jonathan just wanted to be loved. You both apparently moved mountains trying to accommodate everyone so you could get what you wanted—acceptance and love. We'll figure that out in subsequent sessions." Then, he turned to me and said, "If Kelly doesn't feel safe, nothing positive is going to happen. And she certainly doesn't feel safe around you and your anger right now." He certainly wasn't going to hear that most of my anger had always been the result of her abject rejection of me.

Over the next few weeks, talk of divorce was tabled as we saw Kilian often, together and separately. But Kelly wouldn't talk to or see me between sessions. When she came to the house to pick up Sarah, she wouldn't even get out of the car. Kilian commended us for holding the marriage together for as long and as well as we had, given that we each had retreated into our respective bunkers right from the start of our marriage. In joint sessions, he worked hard to make us recognize the roots and nature of our problematic relationship. He elicited from each of us how we had built parallel universes without knowledge of the consequences. He made clear that we needed to understand that there was no *blame* for the marriage's disintegration. We each had our own "stuff;" we each had contributed equally to the toxic dynamics of our relationship.

That was the hardest part for me to grasp. Until now, I'd blamed Kelly for the failure of our marriage. "I mean, she's the one who walked out, isn't she?" I said over and over. Like Janet, he wouldn't let me get away with it.

In my solo sessions, Kilian drilled me on the sources of my fears, anxiety and anger. He was certainly blunt. "You are really fucked up, Jonathan. Are you aware of that?"

I wasn't offended. "I have no doubt," I responded. "I wouldn't be so angry and in such pain if I weren't. Hell, only a fucked up individual could still be so in love with someone who has rejected him so completely for more than 19 months—or for 20 years, as you say. So what are you going to do to help me face it and deal with it?" He responded that change of the magnitude necessary to fix our crippled marriage couldn't happen overnight.

Despite our efforts, it proved too little too late. On April 16, twenty months after firing her first salvo over a bagel, Kelly opened our final joint therapy session with the statement, "It's time to move on." Kelly went on to summarize why a divorce was the only solution. "I feel completely evaporated around you, Jonathan. Your energy is way too strong for me to handle. I feel overpowered, invisible and I disappear in your presence. I am scared to death of you."

I had heard all of this before. But this time there was no barbed edge in her voice, only resignation and pain. "Why?" was all I could muster.

With that, Kilian came flying out of his chair and bent over in front of me, his face no more than a few scant inches from mine. "She has no fucking idea why she feels evaporated and overpowered by you!"

I laughed nervously. "Can I quote you verbatim on that?"

He shot back, "Absolutely. *She has no fucking idea why she feels evaporated and overpowered by you.* Write it down." He got out of my face and returned to his seat. I wrote it down. "What is absolute is that being in proximity to you, the development of an idea is impossible for her. She needs to be completely and thoroughly away from you to heal." When I asked him if that excused her from the years of criticism, condescension and lack of appreciation toward me, he only glared at me.

That evening we told the kids about our decision. In hopes of minimizing confusion, we presented a unified front about what was happening. It took every ounce of restraint for me not to lash out that it was "her" not "we". Given the events of the past year and a half, they weren't very surprised. They were just very, very sad.

Later, as I was drifting off to sleep, lost in loneliness and pain, Alex quietly entered my bedroom and crawled into bed with me. He hadn't done that since he was a toddler. Without a word, he put his arms around me in an embrace that was so tender it would make the strongest of men weep. We hugged and cried for a while. With our hearts wide open to each other, we talked quietly about the divorce and the depths of his pain. Throughout the preceding 20 months of hell, Alex had been the most silent of our three kids. He wouldn't talk about what he thought or felt watching the break up of his parents' marriage. He would only say, "You'll work it out." So hearing him open up was amazing. Painful. Heartbreaking. But wonderful.

* * *

Four days after she asked for a divorce, Kelly had the two of us sitting in front of a mediator. We'd agreed that we didn't want the divorce to get contentious, nor did we think there were any issues we couldn't work out together. Neither of us wanted to hurt the other; we were in agreement over the major issues and were willing to talk through any discrepancies. Mediation seemed the sanest route, with its flat fee arrangement that would cost significantly less than two divorce lawyers.

In this initial meeting, it was explained to us that mediation is a six-step process, spread over approximately six weeks. The first five sessions would involve meetings with a variety of specialists, including a mediation divorce attorney, a CPA, a tax attorney and a family social worker. All issues concerning custody, division of marital assets, child support, alimony and the like would be discussed and resolved. In the sixth session, we would review the draft Divorce Agreement, the document binding us to the terms of our divorce contract. After that, it would be up to us to edit and finalize the document. After we signed this agreement, it would be filed in a court, and a state-mandated 90-day waiting period would follow. We would then receive a piece of paper from a judge saying, in effect, "If you still want to go through with the divorce, sign this document." Once signed and returned, a final Divorce Decree would arrive within 30 days stating we were legally divorced. Whether or not we ever sent in that last piece of paper for filing, the Divorce Agreement itself was valid and the law required us to follow it from the moment we both signed and notarized it.

Almost 21 months into my living hell, a light bulb finally snapped on in my brain. I can't quite put my finger on what flipped the switch. Maybe it was the feeling of finality that attended our impending divorce. Or the months of therapy; the too many days and nights curled up on the bathroom floor; the passage of time; the fact that Kelly was moving no closer to returning to our marriage nor showing any desire at all to try. Certainly, seeing the depth of Kelly's pain played a part. Whatever the reason, I had a moment of clarity that finally permitted me to see and accept our situation. Kelly wasn't in love with me; she wasn't coming back. Given that, I had to give myself permission to move on and make a life without her. And I had to let her go without anger or guilt. That would prove more difficult, since with this newfound clarity came intense heartbreak. I wrote her a letter and sent it as an email attachment. It was the hardest letter I have ever written. It was also the most heartfelt.

> Beautiful Kelly:
>
> So much has come down over these two years. So much learning, growing and hurt. Your pain was so palpable yesterday. It touched my soul in a way that I've never felt before. It was without fear yet with such compassion, love and caring.
>
> So let me fess up in my own words. It is important you know that I "get it." With divorce now a reality, it is more essential than ever to know that it has not all been for nothing. I have been horrible at expressing my understanding through this hell but I can and have integrated it. My big male ego certainly created roadblocks along the way. Yet whatever walls I surrounded myself with, whatever words I didn't use to appropriately acknowledge you and express myself, need to be cleared up. Based on our history, writing seems to be better than trying to talk – at least for now. So please bear with me while I attempt to get my thoughts down on paper. If I ramble a bit, well … I hope you understand.
>
> Yes, we both had to go through this. We were both too co-dependent. I was way too shut off – not just from you, but from just about everything, including myself. Yet there is a connection with you and me that goes way beyond love. That's the part I can't reconcile with this divorce. But I accept your decision and think that I am finally at peace with it. Well, maybe not at peace – how can I *ever* be at peace without you? But I understand the 'why' and can at least accept that. You never felt heard. You never felt accepted for who you really are. You never felt acknowledged by me. I was overpowering; I was defensive. I didn't want to hear your innermost thoughts about you, me and us. In so doing, I shut you off and shut you down. You are scared to be around me, afraid of my responses and the anger in my reactions. You feel evaporated, overpowered, that I'm too strong.

In my presence you feel that you disappear. Being in proximity to me, it makes the development even of an idea impossible. I never heard you. Now I hear you, but it's too little too late.

We never did have 'equal' communication. Part of it was because I didn't know how; part of it was because I felt threatened by it. I had never learned to really see you and honor you for the person you are. I had you shut off and walled in. It is so hard for me to face that fact about myself. But I must ... and I am.

Fear is at the base of this whole nightmare for me. So many fears were buried so deeply. When they came roaring up, I was completely unprepared to handle them. One by one, painful step by painful step, I started to address them. The fear of abandonment, the fear of betrayal, the fear of rejection, the fear of being alone, the fear of being bankrupt (emotionally as well as financially), the fear of losing everything that was important to me. The list goes on and on. What I never took into account was the bigger definition of WHY what I was losing was so critical to my existence. Hell, we started out our relationship as friends. That friendship WAS the basis for our relationship. But the friendship got lost. Now I no longer go home to my best friend. That is the hardest, most painful part of this nightmarish reality. It haunts me. It will always haunt me.

I blamed you for so much. I blamed others. I blamed God. This process has disbanded so many of those illusions. Only now can I stop blaming someone else. I can only look at myself. There is peace in that reality. And it will allow me to divorce without fear – something that petrified me into depression not too long ago.

Kelly, I have such passion for you. But the uncontrolled intensity of my love negated you. In fact, it pushed you to a place where you felt like you ceased to exist. Now I understand that you were *never* able to tell me what you really needed. You reached a point where you just plain felt invisible. I was always so clear about what I wanted, but there were so many things that you were unable to tell me, maybe because I was incapable of hearing them.

Sexually, I was too intense. I determined what you needed but never asked what you liked or what you wanted. It's embarrassing and disgraceful just thinking about it now. You must have felt so often like nothing more than my whore. I never understood that before. It took this kind of tragedy to learn that what *I* think isn't necessarily your reality. We were never a couple sexually. Why? Why did you have such complete control over our sex life – or lack of it? Was it because of your family? Me? Me walking away from you before we were married? I never asked. Shame on me.

What I've learned through all of this, though painfully too late, is that honesty, integrity and open communication, coming from a place of love, can heal anything, especially a marriage. But take any one element out, and you disable and dishonor it. I have dishonored you. I have integrity and tremendous love, but I was unable to communicate appropriately and at times wasn't honest with myself – so how could I be honest with you?

I am sorry for the pain that I have caused you. That you held up for so long is a testament to *your* integrity and attempts to make it work. I was asleep at the switch. Please know that what I am living internally is very different than what I have shown you externally. I am growing up. In connecting with my emotions, I realize how bottled up inside I kept them. I only understand now how very lonely you must have been because of it. I am so sorry that I didn't hear you or see you or feel the pain of your loneliness any sooner. I have such tremendous respect and compassion for what you have done over these 20 months - and 20 years - to try and make yourself (and us) whole. Please forgive me.

I love you. I will always love you.

I am deeply, deeply in love with you. And I always will be.

Jonathan

In this letter, I was able to keep it about me, without blame or anger aimed at her. I wish I could say that I had reached a healing point strong enough to get on with my life. Strong though the feelings were that enabled me to write that letter, they didn't last. In a matter of days, the hurt returned with waves of anger and resentment. My marriage was over. My marriage had failed. I wanted my marriage back. She had committed the ultimate rejection – and it still made me boil.

11. I'M OKAY, I'M NOT OKAY

In the end, I didn't handle mediation very well. I didn't want to be there. Despite the good intentions stated in my letter, I found it impossible to take the sessions calmly and in stride. I showed a face that was angry, hurt and devastated. I was still waiting for her to say, "Just Kidding." It required a conscious effort to remain in my chair and breathe.

Journal Entry

Today was mediation session #3. I thought that I was getting stronger. I hadn't wept or fallen apart in a couple of weeks. Today it all went out the window. Just walking into the Mediation Center set me off. Kelly came in with big smiles and started to small talk while we waited for the mediator of the week. I got so irritated and told her that being in this place was really distasteful and painful so *please* cut out the small talk. I was clear, I just plain did not want to be her platonic buddy, her pal. It's not human to expect it from me – it isn't fair. Her arrogance and self-absorption are just vile.

We wouldn't actually sign and notarize the Divorce Agreement until August 19, a full four months after we started the mediation process, a full two years after Kelly's initial disconnect. In the meantime, I continued to see Kilian weekly, trying to get my arms around what he called my "blind spot." I could never elicit a satisfactory description of what he thought that blind spot was, but I understood that it revolved around my sense of insecurity and inadequacy. It also had to do with my view of Kelly as a wife, mother and love interest. Over and over, Kilian stated that I had built a "story" of what these roles were and how they should play out. When Kelly didn't conform to my preconceived stereotype, I erected self-protective walls. "Those barriers in turn keep you from being who you really are," Kilian said. Bottom line: if I thought better of myself, I wouldn't lean on delusion. I needed to be more grounded and comfortable within my own skin. Time and again, he challenged me to stop clinging to a "myth." Did that suggest that my entire marriage had been built on air? That the life I'd lived with Kelly for the last 20 years was little more than a fantasy? It would be many more months before I could even begin to go there.

In late May, I flew to Raleigh, N.C. to visit my Uncle Bob. Bob is the second of my mother's four younger brothers. Less than a dozen years older than me, Bob and I had recently rekindled a relationship that had lapsed under the pressures of geography, time and life. The previous winter when he and his wife, Suzy (both of whom had grown to adore Kelly early in our marriage) heard through the family grapevine about our marital woes, they went out of their way to visit us while passing through Pennsylvania en route to a wedding further north. At the time, their love and caring was greatly appreciated by both of us.

After that, Bob, god love him, stayed in touch. Through late winter and spring, he and I talked by phone every few days. I came to look forward to his calls. His upbeat spirit and helpful nature became another lifeline for me. His honesty about the turmoil early-on in his marriage was instructive. He told me that he and Suzy had battled a combination of addictions, family issues and marital issues, and had come out the other side stronger, happier and closer than ever before. Bob was candid about what he had learned, and the growth and happiness that had resulted. A believer in the concept of "paying it forward," he had long been mentoring people who suffered from assorted addictions, as well as those on the receiving end of the pain. Bob offered to walk me through his methodology and the lessons he'd learned. He said he'd been listening to me carefully and felt that he could make a difference. I jumped at the chance. It was also an excuse to go hug Aunt Suzy. She gives great hugs!

During my visit with Bob, I learned a few key lessons that I'd been unable to hear from anyone else. Therapists and others had tried, but either I wasn't listening or I just wasn't ready to hear it. Bob made me face the critical first step espoused in AA's 12-Step program. Through question and answer, as well as intimate dialogue, he brought me to a point where I truly understood and admitted that I was powerless over my anger and that my life had become unmanageable because of it. Hell, I blew a marriage over it. What was so hard to understand?

This simple lesson was big for me. After I was able to admit my powerlessness, Bob wouldn't let me blame Kelly for anything, hard though I tried. Taking *complete* personal responsibility for my situation was critical to beginning the process of self-healing. Though I still wanted to blame and lash out, still wanted to make my problems someone else's fault, Bob was somehow able to break through my stubbornness and show me the limitations of my thinking.

For whatever the reason, it sank in. I got it. Well, at least for a while. I have a bad tendency to slip back into old habits way too easily.

We spent the rest of the day getting a fix on my character flaws. He brought me to an emotional place where I could see what a bully I'd been with Kelly. I don't remember how Bob got me there, but it was a very gut-wrenching, tearful realization. I was able to identify so many ways that I had bullied her over the years—not on purpose, but because of some deeply ingrained defensiveness. He wouldn't let me fall back on the finger pointing, identifying all the ways she had abused and criticized and rejected me as excuses for my anger.

Bob said that all problems were caused by fear, resentment and guilt, my bullying included. I pushed back, asserting that resentment and guilt were subsets of fear; *fear* was the source of all problems. That was fine by him.

After that, I was able, without resistance, to look at how manipulative I could be. How I used anger to control others and protect myself. How throughout my life I'd taken the position that the best defense is a good offense. How that strategy had made me such a bully that Kelly did not feel safe around me. I had to let her out of jail; I had to set her free. That harsh reality was driven home late in the day when Bob said, "You can't fix her by blame." Touché.

At day's end, Bob shared a few words of advice and wisdom. "Don't blame yourself. There is no recrimination here. Rather, let go of the history. Loving Kelly as you obviously do means giving her the freedom she so vocally seeks. Love her in a way that encourages her to grow. And when the bully inside of you starts to rear its ugly head," he exclaimed with an uncharacteristic intensity, "keep your damn mouth shut!" He concluded, "Forgive her. Forgive yourself." Amen.

When I returned to Pennsylvania, Kilian reinforced what I'd learned in North Carolina. He reminded me that that I had no internal buoy to navigate such turbulent waters; I needed to stop flailing. He strongly suggested that I start paying attention to my own feelings instead of reacting to Kelly's.

"Stop paying attention to what she says," he instructed. "The only way for her to crawl out from her protective covering and for you to stop reacting to everything she says is through a total disconnection. You have to stop engaging each other. All you've ever been able to do is push each others' buttons. Give it up, Jonathan. You can't control her thinking or her rationale. You'll find that there is wisdom in knowing how much you *cannot* do." He was, in effect, reinforcing Kelly's demand for total separation. Despite my resistance, he made me face that everything I did was aimed at getting Kelly back. I was problem-solving – not being.

With divorce pending, you would think that I'd see that I'd run out my options, and accept his advice. Yet, I continued to resist. Each session with Kilian kicked off the same way. "Why do I fall so totally apart every time I see her?" I'd whine. "Why hasn't my salesman's ego stepped in to protect me and give me a 'fuck you' attitude? You keep telling me my love for her is warped because she satisfies none of my needs. Yet all I do is crumble every time I see her or even just hear her car in the driveway." I usually said all of this in one strained breath.

On July 22, following yet another of these tiresome rants, the great *aha!* happened. I guess Kilian had run out of patience with my relentless self-pity. Coming forward in his chair, he said, "Jonathan, repeat these four words to me: *My marriage has failed.*"

I stared at him. Four simple words. Not a tough request, right? I was paralyzed. No matter how hard I tried, I couldn't get my mouth to open. The tears slowly started to leak out. Kilian was unmoved. He repeated his request. I only cried harder. The cycle went on for 10 seconds, or maybe it was 10 hours; I have no idea. I wept uncontrollably while Kilian waited and intermittently repeated the instruction.

"My marriage has failed," I finally whispered.

"Say it again," he demanded.

"My marriage has failed," I mumbled just as pathetically.

"Again," he repeated.

"My marriage has failed."

"Again."

"My marriage has failed."

He didn't stop until I was able to say those four words without tears and without shame.

Just a dumb little exercise, yet it changed everything. As I rode my motorcycle home after the session, I kept repeating the phrase silently. "My marriage has failed. My marriage has failed." By the time I finished the 23-mile trip, the fog that had clouded my head for two years had lifted. I felt an energy unlike any I'd ever felt before. I didn't understand why. I mean, the exercise was so ridiculous. Yet, somehow, the reality of my situation had finally sunk in.

Still, I was wary. Too many times I'd thought something inside me had changed for the better, only to find myself once again getting angry, falling apart or giving up. So, I just watched myself. As each day passed without anger, I felt better about myself and about life in general. There were bad moments, sure. But they were only moments.

Journal Entry – August 6

Tomorrow is my 21st anniversary. As strong as I'm starting to feel, I don't know if I can handle it. So I'm running away. Having dinner in NYC tonight with [an old girlfriend] before heading out to East Hampton to visit other friends tomorrow morning – my anniversary. Hey, East Hampton is a pretty nice place to hide in summer, isn't it?

Journal Entry – August 9

Kelly called and wanted to finalize the edits to our divorce contract. It ended horribly. She acted like a jerk – but then again, so did I.

She just keeps pushing my buttons and I just keep reacting. It was ridiculous. We should both be ashamed. We still trigger each other so easily.

My marriage has failed.

On August 17th, I took Mike to college. Now *there's* an emotional experience any parent can relate to. While he and I were in the campus bookstore loading up on overpriced textbooks, Kelly called on my cell phone. As part of the divorce agreement, we had our house up for sale. In a tone that for the same effort could have been describing the weather, she told me that an offer on the house that we'd accepted two days earlier had just been rescinded. How was Mike? Oh, by the way, the edits to the Divorce Agreement were complete, four clean copies were made; we should get them signed and notarized tomorrow.

Two days later, a notary witnessed our signing of the four copies. Two were for us; two would be submitted to the judge. I had just signed the dissolution of my dream with Kelly.

Under Pennsylvania law, the marriage that we'd lovingly built over more than 20 years had come undone. Yet, miraculously, I did not. I wasn't hurt or angry, I wasn't half out of my mind. During our visit to the notary, Kelly and I had even made light, pleasant conversation. After two years of wanting my wife back so desperately that I wasn't sure I wanted to live without her, I was fine. Standing there waiting for the notary to finish his paperwork, I even told her that I was writing this book.

It didn't take reality very long to settle back in. The pain wasn't gone and I wasn't fine. It was only two days later that I found myself pouring out my heart (again) to Russ over breakfast at a diner. We were on one of our early morning bike rides, so integral to our summer schedules, so incredibly necessary for my emotional healing. Russ might as well have posted a "Doctor's In" sign on the table. What would breakfast have been without me pouring out the latest "I-miss-her-so-much" diatribe? One thing about Russ, he wouldn't soften his comments or opinions to make me feel better. When he spoke, I'd learned to listen closely.

"Dude, when are you going to face reality?" he began. The smile on his face attested to his caring and sympathy for me and my plight. The intensity in his voice pointed directly to what was on his mind. "Kelly sees things her way, you see it yours. Your realities are incongruous. They don't match up. You just plain look at things differently. The two of you spend so much time and energy trying to convince the other of your own reality. It doesn't blend."

"But Russ," I countered, "I've done everything I can to make my marriage work."

"Does it matter?" came his quick response. "Your frame of reference says that you had a perfect marriage. Kelly's reference point is, 'I don't want to be married to Jonathan but I want to make the marriage work.' Now that she's facing her dissatisfaction, it's a formula that just doesn't add up. Face it man, it never will."

The look on Russ's face told a million tales. It spoke of the serious consequence that I needed to face. It pointed to a reality that I didn't want to see. It reinforced the depth of our friendship. I trusted him so completely – I just didn't like what he was saying. I still couldn't accept the plain fact that Kelly didn't want to be married to me.

"Jonathan, mark my words. Within one year of accepting the end of your marriage and being okay with it, you will thank me. And what will you thank me for? Glad you asked. You're going to thank me for unabashedly saying, "'I told you so'."

"And what is it that you told me, dude?" I asked, matching his playful demeanor.

"Simple. That you found a love that is so much bigger, so much fuller and so much greater than you ever thought possible. Man, you are just being set up by the universe to find the real love of your life. What you had was good. What you've got coming will be overwhelming. Mark my words." His eyes glinted. "You don't have to thank me now. But mark my words. Then just remember to thank me when it comes to pass."

It was with a much lighter heart that I remounted the bike to catch the final hues of a beautiful sunrise.

That weekend, Alex came home from an amazing five-week summer performance program at the Berklee College of Music in Boston. His friends organized a surprise welcome home party for him with my gleeful permission to do it at our house. It was so nice to have my boy back home and the added energy of a house full of spirited teenagers.

Kelly called with a smug challenge in her voice to tell me that she was coming over for the party because it was her son too and frankly, still her house and did I have a problem with that? I'm not sure why she was bucking for a confrontation, but I deflected it and just said, "Sure, come on over." For once I didn't get triggered!

The party was upbeat and full of celebration. Kids don't need a whole lot of excuses to have fun. Someone's been away for a few weeks? Great! Let's party! It's infectious and it was easy to understand why Kelly wanted to be surrounded by it.

We were civil to each other and talked about inconsequential things. We hung out in the kitchen and watched the kids while we talked. I struggled with my emotions. Being around my soon-to-be ex-wife still created such pangs of loss. Breathing was difficult; so was visual clarity. To think that only a week before I thought I was on the road to recovery...

I eventually excused myself and disappeared downstairs in to my basement office to do some writing. I seem to do my best writing when my emotions are vibrating at warp speed. Having just spent time around Kelly trying to act like we were nothing more than casual friends, man was I ever pulsating. It didn't take long for Kelly to follow me down.

Again we talked about inconsequential things for a while but soon turned to the subject of our failed marriage. Kelly drove the conversation down a path about how poorly we had handled our disconnect. Time and again she repeated her now well-worn mantra: "It never occurred to me that we wouldn't work things out."

I listened but didn't respond for several reasons. First, it was so hard for me to hear from her how I handled things; she had it all figured out and was telling me—again. Second, how many times could I tell her that the disconnect was not a "we"? *We* didn't disconnect – *she* did. But I kept my mouth shut because nothing good ever came out of picking at that scab. I even initially held my tongue when she clasped her hands in front of her chest and went off into Woo Woo Land.

I dunno. Maybe it was that fact of our imminent divorce. Or maybe it was simply to turn off the Woo Woo shit. At any rate, I chose this moment to fill Kelly in on the status of this book – at the time still a work in progress. Until that point, I'd shared even the existence of the book with very few people. Writing had been part of my catharsis and very personal. Her hard and fast rejection of me didn't do anything to foster best buddy status in my heart nor any desire to share the workings of a soul she so definitively squashed and abandoned. But sitting there in my home office, having only a week earlier signed away the marriage that had made my life so complete, it felt appropriate to tell her more about it. Well, she responded, she had already surmised about the book – which sort of explained why she had no real reaction to the news a week earlier at the notary. "How did you know?" I asked, curious but certainly not upset by the revelation.

"Is it fiction or nonfiction?" she replied, ignoring my question.

"Nonfiction. Why?"

"Is Laila a real person?" she asked, her back stiffening.

"Whoa. How do you know about Laila?" This was certainly getting interesting.

"Answer my question." Her answer came out as a hiss and had that time-worn bite that could remove chunks of the toughest skin.

"She's real. Why?" I answered quietly.

"How dare you," she wailed. "I'm trying to save my marriage and you're out fucking this girl. Here I thought we were working on the marriage." There it was again—*the* marriage. Needless to say, we got into it pretty quickly from there. I can only say that I was proud of myself for not getting loud, triggered or angry.

I didn't hide or defend anything. I stated why I felt no guilt or shame. She insisted *she* was trying to repair a marriage in crisis. I shook my head wearily and said, "We don't have a marriage, Kelly. You walked out on it long ago." The conversation quickly disintegrated from bad to worse to inane.

Kelly made it sound like she was handling this whole breakup so perfectly. She made the Scott thing perfectly okay because, she explained, "At no time was I comfortable with it, I felt wrong hiding it from you." She went on to say that where she had put everything on the table, I had lied to her. "I'm not hiding anything, Kelly. You betrayed and rejected me. The only thing you wouldn't do was leave – well, until last January. You made it clear that you were not in love with me. You harped often on the fact that you may *never* have been in love with me. You spent months telling me how in love you were with the electrician. You repeatedly told me that you didn't need me anymore and that I should go get my life together. You also instructed me numerous times to go find a woman who could receive my passion and could return it with equal strength."

"You refused separation," she countered. "If you had just let me separate like I had asked, we would have been all right."

The Blame Game. Here we go again. "Kelly, no one kept you from leaving. I slept up at Randy's for three months because I couldn't bear the pain. I never asked your permission – I went because I couldn't sleep at night with you so physically close and yet so painfully far away. As is still the case, there was no indication that you even cared about me, much less had any desire to resurrect our marriage. You continue to clearly state that you are not in love with me. You continue to refuse to touch me, or be touched. You continue to sear me with your constant, 'I may *never* have been in love with you'." By now, my voice was a hoarse whisper. "Why are you blaming *me* that *you* didn't separate from the start? Why do you act like it required my permission? Why do you continue to want to make it seem like this divorce is mutual?"

Ignoring my diatribe, she said in her most superior tone, the one that always pisses me off, "I say again, look at what you have instead of what you don't have." The dime store therapist had spoken.

Round and round we went, until she landed on this: "I don't know how to find my way back. Please help." Her plea was pitiful and rather hollow.

"Then look me in the eyes and tell me you *want* to find your way back," I answered without sympathy. She stared vacantly at me. "Kelly, I was *never* a consideration for you in this process. It is either all your way or not at all. I seem to be the one doing all the changing. Now you say you can't find your way back. Nothing you've said or done during these last two years suggests you even want to try. You still can't look me in the eye and say anything – and I mean *anything* – that says you give a damn about me or *our* marriage. The best you can do is refer to this third party thing you call 'The Marriage', like it's about somebody else."

"I can't give you what you want." she said.

"What I want? All have asked for over and over again is for a shred of hope. You give me none. So I ask again, where's the marriage?"

At that and with no answer, she turned back to my affair with Laila, calling it some pretty choice names. I didn't respond. Instead, I found myself thinking, "Maybe Russ is right. Maybe Kelly and I have such completely different realities that wishing for reconciliation is a pipe dream I need to relinquish."

Reconciliation aside, my curiosity was triggered. I asked, "So how did you find out about my relationship with Laila?" She told me.

"I read all of your emails with her."

"How did you manage that? You have no access to my laptop or email system," I countered.

"I didn't break in to your laptop, Jonathan. How dare you even imply that I would do something as vile as that. No, I read them. You have a folder in the filing cabinet. I was looking for something and found the folder stashed in the back of the bottom drawer."

"Kelly, you *never* go in to the filing cabinets. What were you really doing?" I wanted to know.

She ignored the question, a talent she used quite often when she didn't want to answer a question and asked again, "So all of that was real? You and she did all of those things?"

There were over 400 pages of emails I had printed off. I had done that to use as reference material in writing this book. It never occurred to me that Kelly might find it. On the other hand, I didn't really care. So I took a chapter out of her book and didn't answer the question.

At the time Kelly learned about my affair with Laila, I felt neither guilty nor regretful about my choice. I still don't. In retrospect, however, I see that Kelly and I could have handled more forthrightly the question of whether we'd see other people. We could have had a mature conversation first. We could have set parameters around our separation. Was it okay to date? Was it okay to have sex with other people? Though I see now how such a talk might have spared needlessly hurt feelings, I also see that back at that time, Kelly and I were incapable of such a conversation. Or at least I was. My anger at her Woo Woo talk, sprinkled with her ever-present tone of superiority, over her unrelenting rejection and her high-handed attitude all militated against rational discourse. And … oh yea … the electrician.

In therapy, Kilian pushed me hard to break free of the many myths standing between me and a happier reality. We agreed that I had a huge investment in my marriage. It reflected a lifetime of effort. The harder challenge he posed was whether I was married to Kelly or to an ideal. My image of the all-American family screamed from any which way I looked at it: great wife, great kids, great house, great job. But were my interactions with Kelly based on the actual Kelly in the room—or the image of the ideal wife I held in my mind? How much did my *idea* of Kelly cloud my ability to see the real Kelly? Who did she represent? Wife? Mother? Fantasy soul mate?

While growing up, I'd been taught that creating an image, showing an untroubled face to the world, trumped anything else. Nothing wrong with that, per se. Every family has its dirty laundry; why air it in public? What I was connecting with now, however, was how obsessive my need had become to put on a show that upheld my notion of a perfect image. I'd spent a lifetime focusing on image, at the expense of my emotions. I could now see that a good part of my meltdown following Kelly's rejection was about my inability to put a good face on it for the world—and for myself.

Beyond shattering an image of myself, the break up of my marriage represented the loss of my dreams and hopes. I had such a huge investment in those 20 years. Kilian posited that the act of selling the house broke the "image" story wide open. The house represented a lifetime of my effort, and it was now tumbling down. He challenged me to think hard about how I was going to engage Kelly now that the myth had come apart. He challenged me to think through whether I wanted to continue to take responsibility for her life, especially at the expense of my own. Yes, I was starting to break through some of my lifelong illusions. Articulating them was a giant first step.

Letting go of them was a whole other matter. The idea that I could no longer be image-directed slowly began to sink in. I had to get pragmatic, give up doing what was "right," become clear-headed about my present situation. Maybe now was a time for protecting me, not Kelly.

Kilian posed a series of questions that blew me away. "Jonathan, find out what happens if you don't stay in line. What do you think might happen? Where do you think you're going to go? Have you even considered what stories *you* might have sacrificed by being the ever dutiful child, son, husband?"

Sad though it may sound, it never occurred to me that *I* could choose my own course of being. Could I challenge the ingrained "make 'em happy" story that defined my existence? I had a lifetime of putting the important women in my life first. Doing otherwise had never occurred to me. Just considering that possibility created a different outlook for me. It also created an amazing amount of stress.

To survive in my life, I had sacrificed the ability to think originally or critically. The way I viewed it, my role was—had always been—to try to make the women in my life happy. "What do you want me to do?" and "What should I do?" were deeply ingrained responses that kept the peace. To move against that grain terrified me. It was all I knew.

Once again, the universe smacked me over the head with a timely lesson. It was at this time that I went back to see Sheila, the grandmotherly "intuitive" whose channeled reading early in my nightmare hit so close to home. Upon re-reading my notebooks, it struck me how on-the-money she'd been. Why not try again and this time listen with a more open mind?

Moments into the reading, without prompting from me, she channeled the following:

"Jonathan, you *must* forgive yourself. You didn't drown. You *can* come back and participate in life. It's not about dealing with them. [I took this to mean Kelly and my parents.] You need only deal with what *you* must do with your life. Don't try to make them understand or be any other way than what they are. Don't try to monitor their reactions to your life. That is such a key test for you."

How did she know I was struggling with precisely these issues? She continued.

"They will have their own reactions to what's taking place in their lives as well as yours. The lesson is simple: *release yourself from having to deal with them.* There are so many instances where you invite further friction. You don't need to respond to everything. It has become an addictive part of your personality. You only *think* that you have to deal with things, *think* that you have to fix what's wrong with them. They must learn for themselves and deal with it themselves. It is time to withdraw yourself and go in your own direction. You must let go."

"You will never make it the way you think it ought to be. You can never succeed. There are days when you don't *have* to deal – just let it be. It's *not* about dealing, it's just about being. Release them to make their own mistakes, to see it the way they want to see it. Know that you can't do anything about it. There is a tremendous freeing for you. Remember that there are times you don't need to make 'the call' or respond – you don't need to give your viewpoint at all because it doesn't matter. *Their lives are their own.* It's not about you; it's about their making their own mistakes and moving forward – and for you to learn to make your own mistakes. *Learning to open up and trust yourself, to continue going on your own path – whatever it might be – is critical. It is time to surrender and move forward into your own life.* Don't try to convince them of your viewpoint. Release, forgive, move forward."

A few days later Kilian said, "You seem to base what you say on whether or not you'll hurt someone – in this case Kelly or your parents. It's not clean. It's co-dependent. To make the right deal, you have to be willing to walk away from the table. Do something *now* to move your life forward, but remember that you are not responsible for their 'hurt.' It's time to change the notion that you don't count for much in your own eyes."

It was time, in other words, to seek validation from myself—not from others—for my feelings and actions. It was time to assume responsibility for my own life.

12. ONLY THE BEGINNING

So much time, so little progress. How could I have been so wrong? Wrong about Kelly, wrong about her love for me, wrong about our marriage? How could I have counted so securely on a love that no longer—and perhaps never—existed? Being wrong was more than destabilizing and horrifying for me. It was failure writ large—and that was unacceptable. Kilian said that I lived my life as if I were facing the executioner every day if I didn't do what was "right." I was always trying to be what I thought everyone else wanted me to be, Kelly included. It was the pattern in my life that needed blowing up.

Kilian pushed me hard to face my feelings, stressing that I would not truly be ready for another relationship until I did. How was I so easily deceived? Why did I still want this marriage that didn't work, and want it to be okay? What we agreed was that I had a very strong desire not to be pushed out of the love nest. How could I not be loved in such a profound way by the woman who was supposed to love me "til death do us part?" In essence, how could I have been so wrong about her, about me, about us?

The holidays were not as painful as I expected. The kids and I spent Thanksgiving in Florida at my brother's place. While there, our house went under contract for a planned closing at the end of February. I spent Christmas in Atlanta with Laila and had a blast. She had finally thrown her husband out, and was comfortable with her decision to divorce him. There was no stress, no ugly thoughts of marriages gone awry. For the first time in over two years, I slept soundly, laughed heartily, and enjoyed each moment for what it was. Life could be pretty good. Maybe I was finally waking up.

On New Year's Eve I flew north and arrived home 30 minutes before the ball fell in Times Square. Both Alex and Sarah were there celebrating with friends. It was a wonderful way to ring in the New Year. "I'll be damned," I thought. "Maybe this will be a great year."

And maybe not.

Little J checked in several nights later during yet another sleepless jag. Writing the Little J letter was a little spooky. It was written before I consciously knew what I was doing.

The letter blew me away. I hadn't done this exercise in almost a year. The penmanship and the thought process were light years more mature and healthy than the Little J I knew back when. Though the line about feeling "like I've become so small to her" particularly hurt, I could see that I had finally taken a giant, positive step toward emotional recovery. More specifically, maybe I was finally growing up.

I was also beginning to connect with something very big and very scary: my fear of rejection. It probably stemmed from a style of parenting that brooked neither argument nor dissent. Instead, when discipline was meted out, it came in the form of what my siblings and I called the "silent treatment." Looking back, I can appreciate that it was a style of parenting no less well-intended than my own. But at the time, the long silences felt rejecting, threatening—even obliterating. I would watch one or another of my siblings endure a tortured silence, and think, "No way, not me." I tap-danced fast to please and do the "right" thing. Unconsciously, I shaped my days to avoid confrontation with this most frightening of my demons. As a result, I was never alert to indications that it was time to change direction in my life

Dear Big I -

There is so much going on.
My head is spinning. Sometimes I am
so sad I just want to cry. But there
are times when I feel really happy too.
It's like waves going back and forth.
It's really exhausting.

There are so many lessons being
hurled at us. I feel overwhelmed, but
often excited about where it's going.
I just wish I were smarter and
could understand more of it faster.
Sometimes I think that I am so
dense.

I miss Candace. Why doesn't she
love me any more? What is it I no longer
have to hold her love of me? I feel
like such a failure. I'm not supposed to
fail. I feel like I've become so small
to her.

How will I ever be able to live without
her? We're moving to a new home without
her. I thought we were a family. So
much for that myth.

I still can't sleep. I could if

Candace were here and I could
hold on to her while I slept. but I
also think I could do that with [redacted]
Layla which is nice.

Or I PLEASE figure out why I
really don't want to let Candace go
I think I'm ready. I know it's
fine.

Teach me how not to see all
of this as one big -failure.

I want to grow up now.
Really.

LJ

By pulling away from me, Kelly not only let this demon out for a devastating romp; she stripped away my survival gear. Everyone— myself included—could see the vulnerability that lay at my core. I had nowhere to hide and no one to hide behind. For too long, I'd been pointlessly looking for cover.

Now, I saw, it was time to accept responsibility for my actions and inactions. I had to decide not to blame Kelly or anyone else for my plight. I had to start taking responsibility for myself.

With that realization came a surprising release. I started to feel stronger, less alone, less afraid of consequences. I, who had suffered a life-long dread of solitude, began to enjoy my time alone. I even began to relish it. Until now, I'd been living a life scripted by others. Now, it was time to create my own script. Writing about my experiences offered one sort of release. Motorcycling offered another—probably the more potent of the two. It was so anti-expectation, so antithetical to the authority dynamic I'd learned as a kid and never thought to question. It served no purpose beyond simply this: my own pleasure.

On my motorcycle, I know I am alive. There is only what is in front of me. The beauty of the landscape; the wonderful smells emanating from the farms, rivers and hills of Bucks County and surrounding countryside; the sensation of wind whipping across my body and face; the awareness of the hot air in summer or the bone-chilling cold in the spring and fall. On my bike, life is right there, right in front of my face. There is no yesterday, no tomorrow. There is no Kelly haunting my soul or squeezing the joy out of my being. There is just the open road in front of me. On my bike, I didn't feel depressed or sorry for myself. The motorcycle locks me in to the moment; it is my joy machine.

I respect the bike's raw power and control. It makes me feel small, vulnerable and exposed. Paradoxically, it makes me feel complete.

As I began to accept greater responsibility for my time and sense of well-being, I began to hear with more open ears when Kilian pressed me to connect with my emotions and stop hiding behind "image." By walling off my emotions to avoid confrontation,

I had never learned how to acknowledge and manage the ugly ones—rejection, anger, even rage—that I feared would obliterate me. Instead, I'd leaned for too long on silence, irritation, sarcasm, blame, cynicism, degrading comments. Now, I was finally beginning to see that my self-protective weapons hadn't protected me at all; instead, they'd helped bring about the dissolution of my marriage.

Laila was also instrumental in helping me face my anger. "Jonathan, nobody can accuse you of not wanting to get it right. The huge difficulty is having two people get down to the business of learning how to address what they don't know in order to get it right," she said during one particularly candid conversation. "You are lost in your own sauce. Your notion of life, your place in it and the associated obligations you feel that you need to fulfill have all been thrown into question. Don't minimize or ignore the anger. You should be angry. The question is, how will you handle it going forward?"

I joked often with Laila that I should pay her instead of Kilian for therapy sessions. She knew me like nobody else. She wasn't threatened by me nor was she scared of me. She saw me for who I really was and loved me anyway. "When triggered, you get angry," she mused. "But the anger is just your cover up for the hurt. You need to see that 'lock up' when it happens. You need to let the child, that Little J, emerge. Greet him with tenderness, gentleness and compassion." She was on a roll.

"Be compassionate with yourself when your anger is triggered. See it when it's in your conversation. Feel what it is doing to you. Watch how it is affecting what you say, how you respond and how you interpret the flow of what you systematically but unconsciously go through when triggered. Do it for yourself. Do it for that little kid inside who came to expect no compassion for not towing the line. Sweetheart, you will no longer get punished for not getting in line. You've made that decision. You don't have to play emotional hardball any more."

I listened. I absorbed. I didn't get defensive.

I wasn't—I'm not—quite there yet. Accepting that it's all right to be wrong, believing that I'll survive even if I don't get "it" right and others regard me as a failure, is still tough to swallow. But at least I see now that Little J had it right. I want to grow up. Really.

I've forgiven Kelly—well, at least on most days I do. I understand that there were things she had to do for herself; that probably she never meant to hurt me. More importantly, I've forgiven myself. I fucked up a lot of things in my marriage, but never intentionally, never maliciously.

These days, if Kelly were to ask me, "Do you get it?" I'd finally be able to answer, "Yes, I get it."

But she's no longer here to ask. And that still makes for some very bad days. On my best days, I feel like I've moved on and have a wonderful, exciting life ahead. On my worst, I still ache to hear, "April Fools!" Even on my better days, I still fantasize those words coming from her mouth. Daring to confront my deepest feelings has entailed emotional risk. With the help of therapy and a few good friends and family members, I am stretching beyond my self-imposed boundaries. I've come to realize that holding onto my anger only reinforces Kelly's control over me. I am finally not willing to accept that.

I still bounce like a yo-yo. Good times are more frequent and last longer, bad times are now usually measured in hours, not days or weeks. My heart still refuses to cooperate with what my mind now knows and understands: my marriage has failed.

But good day or bad, I no longer fear being alone. Hell, I am alone—and more alone time is headed my way. We sold and moved out of our house of 15 years on the last day of February. I bought a new residence of my own—my first completely solo—something affordable for me and the kids, nothing special. It's also large enough to permit the comings and goings of my kids' friends, a distraction and comfort that proved so critical to my healing throughout this long journey. And it's my place. Painful as the move was, I actually looked forward to it. It accelerated the process of decoupling from the woman I love.

Or think I love. Hard as Kilian continues to press me, that's the part I still can't get a handle on. "How were you so easily deceived?" he demands. "You live your life as if you're facing the executioner every day if you don't do what's right. Your marriage wasn't right—and the failure still scares you." How many times have I heard him say that? How many more times will it take before I get it?

He doesn't let go of the "story" idea either. "She provided you with the trappings of a life. A story. It's the collusion of the idea of an idyllic marriage that made your relationship last as long as it did."

Whatever. I'm working on it. Hard.

I'm dating now, though I still wish I didn't have to. I feel bad sometimes because although my head tells me what I need to do, my heart still yearns for Kelly. As yet, no woman seems as beautiful to me as the one who left.

I've met several women who are interesting and vital and eager to connect with me. But I'm proceeding slowly, carefully. I don't want to make the mistake of the proverbial rebound relationship. I don't want to hurt anyone, which is proving difficult. I don't want to hurt myself either. That part gets a bit easier with each passing day.

Laila and I continue to talk, often several times a day. We see each other as often as the 800-mile distance permits. She knows what she wants and she's clear that I'm a serious part of her future.

She wants some measure of commitment from me and gives it freely in return. As yet, I'm incapable of returning that commitment. I hurt her with my state of unknowing, and ache that I hurt her, but I know that I'm not yet ready to commit to anyone but myself. At the same time, I'm keenly aware that she knows me better than anybody. She knows all of my phobias and weaknesses. She's seen the worst of me and isn't put off. I know her the same way. I can't help but think that I'm a fool for not seeing what's right in front of me. Then again, I must finally be real with myself – true with finding out who I really am and what I really feel – unimpeded by the pull of that "dominant other", whether it be a parent, my ex-wife or Laila.

I'm still learning to really see and understand what I feel. Only now am I finding the courage to stop hiding behind self-protective barriers and start discovering who I really am. By allowing myself to be weak, I have become stronger. I've also learned that this lesson is not for the faint of heart.

As a result, these days I'm gentler with myself. I was able to articulate the change to Kilian. I told him how powerful my internal changes have become. "I feel calm and at peace with myself," I said. I described my feelings for Kelly, a deep love, without pain or anguish – well, at least most of the time. I described what I wanted in my life. Divorce may not have been my choice, but I now feel content to go forward without Kelly. "Most important," I said, "for the first time in my life, I feel comfortable in my own skin."

When he asked me to describe what I meant by that, I responded, "I'm not afraid of being alone. For the first time in my life, I am completely accountable for my own time. I'm not hiding behind something or someone. I actually look forward to 'alone time,' something that made me panic my whole life. I don't hide behind a television when there's free time. I have hobbies for the first time ever. I'm learning to play the piano. I've bought my own motorcycle. Hell, I bought two! What took me so long?"

I told Kilian how I appreciate things I've never noticed before. Hummingbirds. The fruits of my gardening: every flower, every color, every visual sensation. "I have never felt this energy, this power before," I said. "I can't get out of bed fast enough each morning to experience all that's been in front of me all my life, but went unnoticed. I also don't let my spirit get sucked in to other people's negativity or games anymore. Where I used to get drawn in so easily, now I quite selfishly deflect it. And damn does *that* feel good."

I spoke for 20 minutes. I could have talked all day. My marriage had failed—yet I felt better than fine. There were moments when I even felt euphoric. I ended: "I'm still not over Kelly. There are moments that I still miss her so much it hurts. But I've finally moved on. I know she's not coming back and I know there is a wonderful life still in front of me. It's time to get on with it."

"You're different today, Jonathan," he responded. "I see a substance in you that I haven't seen before. I'm hearing you create a new language that reflects the change. You're not hiding in a territory that's familiar."

My divorce went final just before Thanksgiving.. A journey that was now into its fourth year had some measure of finality. That's what a divorce means, doesn't it? What caught me a little off guard, though, was an email that Kelly sent me. It arrived in my electronic in-basket the week before the final divorce papers came back from the courts making legal the dissolution of our marriage of now 21 years. It ended with, "I deeply respect the pain that we have both endured and the growth that we have both experienced. If there were a way to save our marriage that would bring out the best in us instead of the worst, we should do it." Did she actually say, "our marriage"? Did she actually imply that she wanted to save our marriage? After better than three years of my pleading – no, make that begging – for her to just tell me that she cared? That she gave a damn about us and our marriage? That our union meant something to her and was worth at least trying to rescue? After three years of, "I can't say that," now this? Now?

I had been clear with Kelly that I didn't want a "friendship" with her. It was too painful for me. There was nothing mutual in the divorce and the pain of her rejection was still quite real. Maybe in years going forward that would change. But not now, not yet. That said, I agreed that it was critical to keep an open channel of communication on anything involving the kids, their schedules and their welfare. Yes, we needed to be exemplary co-parents. And I was clear that this was the only kind of ongoing contact that I wanted with her. She couldn't understand my position. "We need to be friends," she kept repeating. I steadfastly disagreed.

So when she asked me out for coffee just after the New Year, she covered it by saying that she wanted to talk about the kids. Over cappuccino, she quickly dispensed with the subject of our family and pushed on to another topic. She said that now that I was strong and didn't need her any longer, and now that she was strong and wasn't scared of me, it was time that we put our marriage back together. She was ready to try again. Her manner was pretty matter-of-fact and businesslike. Certainly, there was nothing tender or inviting in it.

Still, here was Kelly, finally saying what I'd longed to hear for three long years now. That surprised me. But I wasn't surprised to hear myself say, "No thank you." Nor was I surprised by the certainty and ease with which I said it. I had moved on.

Bad as I still feel sometimes, my protective walls are down. After 21 years of living in the story of a perfect marriage, that fiction is no longer acceptable. My entire perception of reality has been dismantled. For more than three years, a raging river had dragged me through its roiling waters, scraping and battering me along the way. Now, I've let go. Most days, I let the power of the river carry me. I am - and you know what it costs me to say this - living in the present. I feel no impulse to apologize for or try to fix yesterday. I have no inclination to try and manhandle an outcome for tomorrow. I'm not stuck on the importance of what other people think. Instead, I am basking in the calm waters that follow a violent storm. Now, I realize, I can swim to a shore of my own choosing. I finally understand—in my heart as well as my head—that I am the *only* person who can make me happy.

I lost my wife, yes. But somewhere along the way, I found me.

ACKNOWLEDGMENTS

To Jill – my sister, friend, confidant, editor, inspiration and role model. Thank you for your love, caring, sharing, unwavering belief in me and persistence in helping me to grow, even during my extended stretches of self-pity. Without you this book never would have happened. Without your unflagging love and attention, I may *never* have gotten through this mess.

To Michael, Alex and Sarah - my beautiful kids. If you only knew the strength you gave me through the worst of it. I hope you know the joy you bring me each and every day. I love you guys more than life itself.

To Alan – Bro, your unfaltering love and support were so critical to my survival. Thank you for being there for me every step of the way.

To Gatha – "*Hello Gatha Cash. It's Monday!*" Because of you, I now know that unconditional love *is* possible. I also know that Monday has become my favorite day of the week.

To Russ Reed – What can I say to the friend who was there for me right from the start? You held me up when no one else could. You made me laugh when no one else would. You taught me how to play, even in the worst of it - what an amazing gift. Thank you for not giving up on me and instead teaching me how to live every day to its fullest. You're my hero. [*Author's note: my extraordinary buddy, Russ, passed away prior to publication. I miss him deeply. He will always be my hero*]

To Laila – You're amazing. Thank you for caring so darn much … and not giving up on me.

To Bob Andron – Uncle Bob, I am so grateful you came back into my life when you did. You've taught me so much and inspired me even more. I'm still working on the "forgiveness" piece, but I'll get there. I promise. I cherish you and Aunt Suzy. Blaze on, baby!

To John Volpe – What can I say? You were right …

To all of the amazing people who supported me through my experience in so many ways and by giving me feedback on the book at every stage, including Dr. Vera Frumin, Dr. Paula Elbirt, Dr. Kilian Fritsch, Dr. Nancy Newman (Newms!), Lilly and Mark Bartholomew, Robert Friedman, Ph.D, Nancy Lothrop, Valerie Wilkinson, Elaine Feldman, Kumani Gantt, Mim Klein, Babette Sutherland and Vytas Kisielius. Thank you all for your love, friendship, indefatigable support and editorial comments.

And most of all, to Kelly.

ABOUT THE AUTHOR

Jonathan Lewis has over 33 years of experience in technology sales and marketing, starting with 12 years at IBM. A graduate of Princeton University with a BA in economics, he's spent the last two decades happily ensconced in the world of start-up companies. Jonathan is the proud father of three grown children.

You can communicate with Jonathan via email: 19Jonathan.Lewis56@gmail.com

Made in the USA
Columbia, SC
14 October 2021

47190178R00130